A SEARCH FOR CLARITY

Series Editors

Slavoj Žižek

Adrian Johnston

Todd McGowan

diaresis

A SEARCH FOR CLARITY

Science and Philosophy in Lacan's Oeuvre

Jean-Claude Milner

Translated from the French by Ed Pluth

Northwestern University Press
Evanston, Illinois

Northwestern University Press
www.nupress.northwestern.edu

Originally published in French in 1995 under the title *L'Œuvre Claire:
Lacan, la science, et la philosophie.* Copyright © 1995 by Editions du Seuil.

Printed in the United States of America

10 9 8 7 6 5 4 3 2 1

Library of Congress Cataloging-in-Publication Data

Names: Milner, Jean-Claude, author. | Pluth, Ed, translator.
Title: A search for clarity : science and philosophy in Lacan's oeuvre / Jean-
    Claude Milner ; translated from the French by Ed Pluth.
Other titles: Œuvre claire. English | Diaeresis.
Description: Evanston, Illinois : Northwestern University Press, 2021. | Series:
    Diaeresis | "Originally published in French in 1995 under the title L'œuvre
    Claire: Lacan, la science, et la philosophie"—Title page verso. | Includes bib-
    liographical references.
Identifiers: LCCN 2020032853 | ISBN 9780810142848 (paperback) | ISBN
    9780810142855 (cloth) | ISBN 9780810142862 (ebook)
Subjects: LCSH: Lacan, Jacques, 1901–1981. | Psychoanalysis and philos-
    ophy. | Science and psychology.
Classification: LCC B2430.L146 M55 2021 | DDC 150.195092—dc23
LC record available at https://lccn.loc.gov/2020032853

Contents

Introduction

I do not intend to clarify Lacan's thought. I have neither the authority nor the qualifications to do so. Moreover, clarification does not appear to be especially urgent. Lacan is, as he said himself, a crystal-clear author. He just has to be read carefully. Of course his readers would like guides, but there are serious institutions and excellent works already offering them. Truly, the Lacanian bibliography is distinguished by the quantity and quality of its titles. Given our current needs, the commentaries available to us today are already perfect, with the following qualification: the better ones are neither the most accessible nor the best known.

True, a Lacan according to the order of reasons does not yet exist.[1] But it took two centuries for Descartes to be read according to the principles that he himself had formulated. And Kant needs to be reread carefully in every era. The scholastic form he inherited from Wolff was very constricted, but it did not protect him from being misread. So we can assume that someday, soon perhaps, a return to Lacan will have to be made, just as Lacan himself had to make a return to Freud. Reading errors are to be expected and are no doubt inevitable: they are a regrettable part of fate. They simply have to be given some time to become apparent. In France anyway, there has not been enough time for that (I would not say the same about the Americas, but I am not writing for them).

This is not an attempt to present Lacan in a way that grasps his work according to its inner logic—whether this is consistent or not—nor is it trying to put forth his work in such a complete way that any possible misinterpretation of it is corrected. My intention is entirely different: not to clarify Lacan's thought, nor to correct what has been said about it, but simply to establish clearly, for the record, that there is a thought in Lacan. A thought—that is to say, something whose existence imposes itself on those who have not thought it.

Those who are interested in accuracy and clarity assume that this thought's existence is given. They are right to do so. They also assume that the best approach is for them to clarify Lacan by Lacan; and once again, they are right to do so. Of all the works on Lacan, the most flawless elucidations follow this principle. But if the thought's existence is not assumed to be given, we have to go about things another way.

Propositions are the only valid supports for a thought's existence. To say that there is a thought in Lacan's case is thus to say that it contains propositions. But nothing exists without having properties, and nothing has properties that are not, at least partially, independent of their context. So it is necessary to establish that in Lacan's thought propositions exist that are robust enough that they can be taken out of their context and withstand changes in position and modifications to their discursive space. It is also not necessary to be exhaustive; it suffices that some of these properties are found in some propositions. Put this way, my program is defined by its externality and incompleteness.

I intend to reconstruct only some interconnections, and I do not intend to put them back together into a whole that would claim to shed light on the general construction of Lacan's oeuvre (we will see in what sense the word "oeuvre" is to be understood here). For example, I will emphasize the importance of the question of science. We know that Lacan emphasized this question; nevertheless, it is not the case that the totality of fundamental psychoanalytic concepts, in all their detail, can be deduced from it. Moreover Lacan, on this question, does not stop not authorizing himself from himself. It is as if the question of science were so decisive that he had to go back to it repeatedly, and as if at the same time it was sufficiently foreign to what was essential to him that the work of an external guarantor—namely, Koyré—sufficed. In a similar way, the paradigm of structural linguistics took on a well-known importance, and yet no one could ever convince himself that Lacan was familiar with the works that belonged to this discipline: it was as if their pure and simple existence sufficed, providing an external buffer zone that closed off and protected the places to be conquered.

But I claim that this is a good use of externality. Lacan himself made use of it, so it is legitimate to apply it to his work.

The Lacanian doctrine on science comes from Koyré, but it uses Koyré for purposes that were foreign to him. Because of this fact, it contains properties of Koyré's doctrine that are often only latent in his key texts. In the same manner, Lacan is able to bring out some properties of structuralist doctrine precisely because he keeps himself in a paradoxical position of external inclusion from it. If, by contrast, we start with the doctrines of science and structure, making an effort to reveal the theses that distinguish Lacan's thought for themselves, the externality of these doctrines will help us better approach the natural location of Lacanian propositions; in this way, objective and quasi-material properties will emerge.

Lacan said that in order to bump into the walls you do not have to know the floor plan. Better: to encounter the walls where they actually are, it is better not to know the plan, or if it so happens that one does know it, it is better not to take it into account. There are two ways of recognizing an object's shape. One of them starts from the object's interior and, on the basis of a law or a combination of laws, generates its contours. This is what a geometrician is doing when tracing a circle, and this is what a linguist is doing when constructing a grammar. The other way starts from the outside, takes the presence of nearby bodies into account, and establishes how these bodies, due to their lateral position, determine the shape of the space in which the object is placed. This is what rivers and cities do, which are materially organized by the obstacles that surround them and ignore them. I've chosen the second path here: to describe some of the mountain ranges surrounding Lacanian discourse that it collided into, circumvented, and eroded away, not without being shaped by them, and not without shaping them either. This may be called a discursive materialism.

After all, this is exactly what legitimates the reading techniques that are so characteristic of Freud and Lacan. Shift the accents in order to make the real of the rhythmic matrix better understood. Break away from visible connections, in order to shed better light on the real ones. Get rid of significations, of their explicitness and completeness, in order to make the (always incomplete) sense emerge.

Again, it is not necessary to be exhaustive. Admitting the externality of its point of view, a discursive materialism can consider itself satisfied, and its program completed, as long as some properties of some propositions will have been found. It will be no surprise, then, that on manifestly basic points regarding internal doctrinal logic, hardly anything will be said here. Neither desire, nor object *a*, nor the phallus, nor, in a general manner, anything that justifies the existence of clinical statements will be taken up. But if something is missing, this is not due to an oversight, especially not if what is missing is indispensable.

The greatness of all authentic materialisms is that they are not totalizing. It is by accident that *De natura rerum* and *Capital* are incomplete, and, for this very reason, a systematic necessity emerges. Their incompleteness allows them to be treated in a partial manner. Non-totalizing readings are appropriate for non-totalizing works. If the greats can be compared to each other, the Lacan I am proposing here will turn out to be confirmed if he is revealed to be as incomplete as Lucretius or Marx.

Ultimately, no personal commitment should be perceived here. Neither doubts nor hopes. Neither admiration nor disdain, nor indifference. Neither remembrance nor forgetting. I have deemed it inappropriate to express what I personally think about Lacan or, thanks to Lacan, about the conjuncture he was part of, and that he sheds light on. It has been necessary to adopt the point of view of a flow of water when shaping a landscape. It is not necessarily the case that I don't think anything at all about what I am talking about—I have been open about this in other contexts—but a personal thought here would not be pertinent.

If it ever is. I am in fact more and more convinced that thought is something too serious to leave to people, except under extraordinary conditions. Lacan is undoubtedly one of the exceptions. There are some others. By definition, they all only have their worth because of their rarity. In any case, they spare those who speak of them from demanding any consideration for themselves. If there is to be any thought in the current discourse of the world, I take it as an acceptable ethical maxim that one should act in such a way that there may be as much of it as possible. This also implies that its existence should impose itself on the greatest number of thinking beings possible. This is, truly, the only justifiable reason for any text to exist, rather than not. With one condition, however: that, without exception, the thought be only that of objects.

A SEARCH FOR CLARITY

1

Considerations on an Oeuvre

What is usually called Lacan's oeuvre appears in two forms. On the one hand there are texts written by Lacan for publication; on the other hand there are the seminars, transcribed and edited by people other than Lacan—some of them under Lacan's direct supervision. The texts prior to October 1966 were collected into a volume entitled the *Écrits*, and the most important later texts—but not all of them—were published in the review *Scilicet*. I take all the texts written for publication to have the same status, whatever their date or location, and I will take the liberty of calling them, altogether, the *Scripta*. Numerous disputes have arisen regarding the seminars. For fundamental reasons, which will appear shortly, I will stick to the edition currently being published with Seuil, entitled *Le Séminaire*, with each volume constituting one book (identified by a roman numeral and a title) of the entire set.

It is impossible not to wonder about the relationship between these two masses of texts. In fact, this amounts to wondering about what is called Lacan's oeuvre. Not only about what composes it materially, but more radically about what authorizes us to speak of an oeuvre in Lacan's case. I have acted as if this question were simple, but it deserves careful examination.

The notion of an oeuvre is modern—if, at least, we take it in a strict sense, as a principle of uniqueness that allows a counting and a differentiation to take place among the multiplicity that is culture.[1] The uniqueness is based on a system of nominations—the name of the author and the title of the oeuvre—that submits material productions, especially texts, to the regime of the One. Whether there are one or several texts is, moreover, entirely secondary, since it is the naming itself that makes them into One: in other words, an oeuvre is not necessarily *a* book, nor even necessarily a *book*. An oeuvre is not a matter, it is a form, and it is a form that organizes culture.

A consistent Marxist would hold that, in the order of thought, an oeuvre is equivalent to what the commodity form is in the order of things. Just as the wealth of societies in which the capitalist mode of production prevails appears as an immense collection of commodities (one will recognize here the first sentence of the first book of *Capital*), culture, for moderns, appears as an immense collection of oeuvres. Each of them counts as one thanks to the guarantee that its uniqueness receives from the association between an author (generally named, but anonymity is an admissible variant) and a title (generally given by the author, but not always). For writings this association is settled by publication, which shows the homology between the oeuvre and the commodity: just as there are only commodities because there is exchange, there is only an oeuvre in the strict sense because of publication.

It has not always been this way. But in modern times, the configuration that has just been described prevails and even extends, *mutatis mutandis*, to all parts of culture; different arts are henceforth subjected to the oeuvre form, each one determining for itself what counts as the equivalent of publications (theatrical performances, exhibitions, television broadcasts, censorship, etc.). It is possible for someone to avoid this configuration, but there is a price to pay: giving up on being part of culture. We can call this "madness"—this is how Foucault's definition should be understood: madness as the absence of an oeuvre. At the same time, this defines madness as the external limit of culture. This obviously does not mean that culture does not have the ability to reabsorb the works madness produces: all it has to do is inscribe them into the oeuvre form. But, once that happens, the term "madness" would no longer be pertinent. It is well known that examples of this abound, and the label *art brut* was invented for no other reason.

However, this is the case not only with madness, with its procession of sufferings and dramas. Contrary to what one might think, vast swaths of modern writings exist in tranquility outside of the oeuvre form—those that fall under the heading of science and its partner, technology. This is how the persistent belief that neither science nor technology belongs to culture should be taken. Far from it being necessary to denounce this as a prejudice on the part of simpletons or humanists (these have not always been the same thing), we need to see the structural relationship at work here: the mutual exclusion of two systems that define themselves by this very exclusion. Consequently, what counts in science does not fit into the oeuvre form; this form, it is true, does apply to it now and then, but at a later date, when the science in question has stopped being efficacious. Einstein counts as an oeuvre only once science determines that, having fully absorbed him, it has the right to forget him. Only then does culture, which is outside of science, come along to make up for the systematic amnesia of the developing sciences, which are outside of culture.[2]

Thus it suffices for a modern thinker who finds himself drawn to both science and culture to be confronted with the question of the oeuvre, and for a decision to have to be made about it. The choice between the two has sometimes been a critical one. This was what was at stake for Saussure's students. We know that they chose the oeuvre form, believing that a collection of scientific works alone would not suffice to preserve the proper name of the one to whom they were attached. Whence the birth of this "organic whole" called the *Course in General Linguistics*, without anyone knowing if the original title was meant to be singular or plural.[3] We know that the editors succeeded by virtue of the fact that everyone uses the singular (we say *the* Course); from then on Saussure is certainly an oeuvre, constituted by the association of the author's name and a text, seen as one entity; after that, Saussure finds his place in culture.[4]

Freud had to make the choice for himself. He even had a strategy; it is as if he preferred to take a detour through the oeuvre form in order to bring about what properly scientific publication prevented him from doing. The dream of the botanical monograph is worth considering from this perspective. "I had written a monograph on a certain plant. The book lay before me and I was at the moment turning over a folded color plate," etc. (Freud 1953a [1900]: 169). The associations revolve around a failure: "Once, I recalled, I really *had* written something in the nature of a *monograph on a plant*, namely, a dissertation on the *coca-plant* . . . which had drawn Karl Koller's attention to the anaesthetic properties of cocaine. I had myself indicated this application of the alkaloid in my published paper, but I had not been thorough enough to pursue the matter further" (ibid., 170). Koller received the glory and the success to which the commemorative volume Freud had received that very morning attested. Freud then thinks with some melancholy about his own book (the *Traumdeutung* itself), which he was slow to finish: "if only *I* could have seen it lying finished before me!" (172). Finally, he evokes his own youthful passion for books: "I had developed a passion for collecting and owning books" (172).

His interpretation: the monograph and the book are in a relationship of conjunction/disjunction; the dream spells out his renunciation of the monograph, that is, of normal science, with its jubilees and laboratories. Preference is given to the book, that is, to the oeuvre form and to culture. The *Traumdeutung*, as a book, will testify to this. In fact, the monograph and the book are part of the same paradigm—this is why the first can "represent" the second—but, because they are part of the same paradigm, they are as opposed to each other as two phonemes are. Their opposition repeats, at the level of the oeuvre, the opposition between science and culture. Freud set out trying to conquer biomedical science (*flectere Superos*); to this end he used the monograph as his weapon; but he was rejected, or he was at least neglected. His initial strategy had to be replaced by a new one that used the book, but the book is just the empirical witness to the oeuvre form, entered into the burial ground of culture (*Acheronta movebo*).

We know what happened next: culture proved strong enough to impose itself on science and medical techniques. The oeuvre form conquered the monograph.

Not without a very heavy price: this was the "wild bunch" that Freud had to settle for, he who had dreamed of the laboratory, of honest scientific collaboration, of faithful students and jubilees. We know that Freud did all he could to make psychoanalysis conform to normal science. The conquest of the modern universe required this. The International Psychoanalytic Association (the IPA) was the preferred vehicle for this strategy.

It is doubtful that this would have been appropriate for a normal science; in many respects, normal science is distinguished precisely by the fact that it is robust enough not to need to *create* such institutions. The clarity of its paradigms, together with the inherited network of medieval universities and, let's say, of the church, were enough to determine everything. In fact, the IPA with its seven rings calls to mind something more like stadium sports—the five Olympic rings—and their authoritarian federations than science.[5] Nevertheless, we can be sure of this: as exorbitant as it was with respect to the good practices of normal science, the International—at least according to Freud—was needed as a stand-in for such practices. Its charter could be put this way: there will never be another oeuvre apart from Freud's, in psychoanalysis or in science; there will only be monographs.

Lacan, too, had to choose. At the end of the Second World War, the IPA had succeeded; psychoanalysis had become part of the organizational universe of normal science, and like any science worthy of the name in the modern universe, it had produced its own technique. Was it then necessary that he limit himself to the monograph? We know that, more astute, and more truly modest than many others, Lacan hesitated on this. Sometimes in favor of silence: "Like Fontenelle,"[6] he writes in 1946, "I gave myself over to the fantasy of having my hand filled with truths all the better to hold on to them" ("Presentation on Psychical Causality," Lacan 2006b, 151). Also in favor of the scholarly journal: this was his model for a long time—*La Psychanalyse* strongly resembles the dignified and brief undertaking of *Recherches Philosophiques*, with which Lacan happened to be associated in the 1930s. But this model is diametrically opposed to that of the oeuvre: any journal worthy of the name falls under the monograph form.

Now, the *Écrits* are published within the framework of the oeuvre. Lacan thus chose. At the same time, he affirmed that there would be at least one more oeuvre in psychoanalysis. This gesture was all the more surprising since it went against Lacan's own trajectory.

Lacan developed the theme of "*poubellication*."[7] It entails a position on the oeuvre: it holds that publication belongs in the dustbin, that the published amounts to rubbish; since there is no oeuvre except in a published form, the conclusion is that any oeuvre, as such, amounts to rubbish. A theory of civilization can be found here, too, coming from Bataille: to belong to civilization, in contrast to the barbarian who refuses it or the madman who exempts himself from it, is to know how to deal with trash and excrement. Culture as an element of civilization, the oeuvre as an element of culture, publication as a dimension of the oeuvre, paper as the preferred medium for both the published and feces: all can be understood in this light. The fact that rubbish is the same thing as the spark needed to attract desire is certainly important (consider the theorems of object petit *a*), but it is not important here.

So then, Lacan agreed to be published; that is, he consented to the oeuvre form; that is, he consented to the trash bin. He must have had serious reasons for doing so.

Only the exclusions of 1963 possess the importance necessary for this. Once again, normal science closed its doors, albeit by faithless imitators; once again, it was necessary to turn to culture in order break the seals; once again, Orpheus had to sing in order to cross the Acheron. This is what the *Écrits* of 1966 are a response to: the book, in its most classical form.

Like Freud before him, Lacan needed culture in order to make himself heard. More clearly than Freud, he knew that this was to choose the route of the funereal and the rubbish heap. Not only because of the tombstone that each book represents, with its cover, like an epitaph, bearing the name of an individual, his titles (the text's taking the place of all the others), a date, a location; not only because of paper being like a cadaver (*caro data vermibus*),[8] but also because of what has no name in any language: the book as an operator of forgetting (*poublier*, Lacan also said).[9] More overtly than in Freud's case, the choice was necessitated by the explicit decision of an Authority.[10]

Lacan succeeded against the International Psychoanalytic Association. We can affirm that there is, in psychoanalysis, at least one oeuvre other than Freud's: Lacan's. This is what marks Lacan's true victory, and the true defeat of the International. I do not have to take a stand on the empirical question of knowing whether there will be other oeuvres. I do not have to take a stand on the theoretical question of knowing whether an oeuvre can cease to be one. It only remains to be established what it is in Lacan's case that makes up the existence of an oeuvre.

Is Lacan's oeuvre the collection of publications, the *Scripta* and *Seminar*, taken together as two wholes? Or is it the collection of *Scripta* alone, or even just the one volume, the *Écrits*? Is it, on the contrary, just the series of seminars? Underneath the petty quarrels that have broken out over these issues, there is a real question.

For a long time I believed that Lacan's *Seminar* was an oeuvre, and that it was in fact the only real oeuvre by Lacan. Thus I agreed with the title that its editor had given it—using a singular substantive and a definite article; I agreed that the sections of the whole should be presented as numbered and titled "books" and that the subdivisions of these books should not be presented as "sessions" or "lessons" but as chapters, themselves numbered and given a title; that these chapters should in turn be subdivided into parts, and numbered as well. I agreed with the project of publishing the text according to the most tried-and-true rules of Erasmian philology (exhaustiveness, precision, exactitude), because philology is at one with the emergence of the oeuvre: it gives the status of an oeuvre to what it deals with, when, at least, it does deal with one (thus Erasmus had to submit the Evangelists to the oeuvre form as soon as he submitted them to the rules of philology, and this is what made him into an impious radical in the eyes of Luther). Similarly, the oeuvre form needs philology in order to be assured of its grasp on the text in question (the oeuvre of a contemporary—Breton, Proust, Attali[11]—will be established as an oeuvre once the classical philological problems regarding it have been raised and settled: dates, editions, classification of variants, dismissal of imitations and derivations, etc. This is usually the job of La Pléiade.)[12]

Still, something did not seem right. What kind of oeuvre, in the strict and modern sense, is so directly linked to an oral teaching and to an explicitly announced annual schedule? What is the relationship between the *Seminar* and the *Scripta*? If the latter fall under the heading of an oeuvre, despite their multiplicity with no discernible order, could it be in the same respect? And if they did not, what were they?

The most cogent precedents are found in antiquity. Taken together, Plato and Aristotle had also produced comments and writings that fell under two different headings. Ancient documents, certainly, but philology, such as it was constituted in the Renaissance, and culture, such as it was constituted in the nineteenth century, based themselves on a principled anachronism: whether true or false, it was necessary to act as if antiquity was also subject to the oeuvre form. This justifies the analogy.

But to think of Plato and Aristotle was also to think of the combination of two distinctions: the distinction between written and oral teaching, on the one hand, and the distinction between exoteric and esoteric writings on the other. If the relationship between the two distinctions is allowed, we can establish the following: the exoteric is written, the esoteric is oral (and eventually transcribed).

We know that the question of the esoteric was important to Lacan, who often evoked the famous lecture on the Good, the core of what a certain tradition maintains was the secret and non-written teaching of Plato. Likewise, he took a keen interest in the question of the lost Aristotle,[13] which can be summarized this way: the majority of what Aristotle wrote is lost; these texts were most often written as dialogues, and were considered wonders of the Greek language; they developed an exoteric teaching; what we read under Aristotle's name was not written by him and is the transcription, by students, of his oral and esoteric teaching. On this basis we can contrast Plato and Aristotle: we have the entire exoteric writings of the first, and nothing of his esoteric writing (assuming that it existed); of the second we only have his esoteric oeuvre, apart from some exoteric fragments that were preserved in the manuscript tradition.

This contrast, familiar to everyone, foreshadows in some respects what distinguishes Freud from Lacan: since we only have writings from Freud, we only have his exoteric work (the *Transactions* of the Vienna Society, published later, do not seem to tell us anything all that new); since we have not only writings but an oral teaching from Lacan, we would thus have from him two sets of teachings: the exoteric one of the *Écrits*, and the esoteric one of the *Seminar*, whose material weight continues to increase over the course of the years.

True, the distinction between the exoteric and esoteric is anything but clear. From a descriptive point of view, there is generally agreement on this: Aristotle's exoteric teaching is addressed to those who are *outside* of philosophy (*exô*) and who have not (yet?) chosen the theoretical way of life. The esoteric teaching is addressed to those who are *in* philosophy (*esô*): they have chosen the proper way of life and have already gone down the appropriate path. Conceptually, there could thus be nothing in the exoteric writings that is more complete, more precise, or more clear, than there is in the esoteric transcripts. Conversely, there could be more completeness, more precision, and more clarity in the esoteric transcripts. If there is something additional in the exoteric writings with respect to the esoteric transcripts, it would not involve conceptual content but would be due to something else whose name we know: *protreptics*, a discursive procedure whose function is to tear the subject away from *doxa* and towards *theoria*. This is the very thing that Aristotle, according to the ancients, did and perfected (see W. Jaeger, *Aristotle* [Oxford: Clarendon Press, 1955 (1934), chapter IV, 54–101]). This is also what, according to some moderns, Plato's dialogues were trying to do.

All this being admitted, I held that Lacan's *Seminar* was, relative to the *Scripta*, what the texts we still have by Aristotle were relative to the lost Aristotle (or what the lost teaching of Plato was relative to what we still have by Plato): it was esoteric, while the *Scripta* were exoteric. So I concluded that the *Seminar* was indispensable for the interpretation of the *Scripta* and, consequently, for the completion of the oeuvre. Since the publication of *The Seminar* was incomplete, this meant that the oeuvre was too; because of this fact, no interpretation of it could claim to be definitive at all; nothing in the *Scripta* would be able to clarify *The Seminar*; only *The Seminar* could, by rights, clarify *The Seminar*, and one could only use the *Scripta* to make conjectures about the not-yet-published part of *The Seminar*.

In this respect, I found myself in agreement with every other interpreter. Some went further; they did not hesitate to claim that as writings the *Scripta* were inferior to the spoken teaching—the famous Spoken Word [*Parole*], which since Socrates or Jesus Christ is what attracted disciples, and was thought to contain an incomparable treasure. Whence the unending commentaries on marks of oral speech, which were thought to be constitutive of *The Seminar*. From this one passes easily into Presence and the figure of a Master, with respect to whom one makes an Apology, whose Trial, if not Passion, are commemorated, and whose memorable sayings or gestures are recorded.

Today, after having read attentively and multiple times what has been published of *The Seminar*, I can claim that I was mistaken. Lacan's seminars are exoteric and not esoteric; it is the *Scripta* that are esoteric—in the sense that Aristotle's corpus is. The first is a web of protreptics—allusions, literary or scholarly flourishes, diatribes, deconstructions of *doxa*; while the second tends to be stripped of such things. The first aims to grab hold of the listener (the transcription puts the listener into the material situation of a reader, but this doesn't make a difference) at the imaginary point the present conjuncture has put him in; having grabbed hold of him, it seeks to dislodge him from his natural location by a violent movement which, in Lacan, in contrast to Plato, takes on the form of diatribe, if not invective: monological and impolite dialogues.[14] The second can certainly behave like protreptics, but what is decisive about them is indifferent to protreptics: the reader (who has far more to do than to put himself into the situation of a fictitious listener) has to decode, and often read between the lines, an element of knowledge.

It is true that the seminars are addressed to analysts and analysands. Because of this, one might suppose that they would have the type of internal closure that characterized esoteric material in the ancient Greek schools. However, Lacan thinks his listeners have not succeeded in occupying their proper position in analysis. The general goal of each particular seminar is to ensure that the analyst situates himself as an analyst and the analysand as an analysand, and that each truly enters into analysis. This entails a movement that is quite precisely analogous to the one that, in protreptics, makes someone go from being outside (*exô*) of *bios theoretikos* to being inside it (*esô*). In the *Scripta*, this movement is assumed to have already been successful.

There is in Lacan's case, then, as in Aristotle's, both esoteric and exoteric material; there is also the written and the spoken. But, from Lacan to Aristotle, the relationship is reversed: the esoteric is written, and the exoteric is spoken and transcribed. So we must conclude the following: from the point of view of thought, there is nothing and will never be anything more in the seminars than there is in the *Scripta*. But there can always be something more in the *Scripta* than in the seminars. There is nothing in the seminars that can modify the interpretation of the *Scripta*, and everything in the *Scripta* is relevant for the interpretation of the seminars.

There is an inevitable consequence of this for Lacan's oeuvre. If such an oeuvre exists, it is entirely in the *Scripta*. But, by definition, all of the *Scripta* have been published. In other words, the oeuvre already exists in its entirety at the very moment I am writing this, even though the publication of the seminars is not complete.

The grammatical singular and the definite article in the title *The Seminar* should not be read as the marks of an oeuvre. They only designate the unity of an institution that was continued in different places over the years. If one thinks, however, of the transcribed texts, the plural would be more appropriate; so I will speak instead of *the seminars* [*des seminars*]. On the other hand, the grammatical plural of the name *Scripta* is due only to the material dispersion of the texts: we must not let it prejudice our view on the existence or inexistence of the oeuvre, which should only be decided on the basis of thought.

Who would not wish to be able to read all of Aristotle's dialogues? Similarly, the publication of all the seminars is of an incomparable documentary importance. That it could ease our access to the *Scripta* by means of protreptics, however, is not certain; because protreptics are circumstantial, and when the circumstances have changed they can create obscurities. This is what has happened with Plato's dialogues, whose exoteric content has made them obscure. It is thus possible that the seminars will make the *Scripta* obscure (just as, after all, the *Theodicy* is less clear than the *Monadology*, the *Prolegomena* less clear than the *Critique of Pure Reason*, or Flaubert's Correspondence less clear than *Un Coeur simple*, or the *Pastiches* less clear than the *Recherche*). No one will contest the fact that they can be a source of lively interest, but we should not be mistaken about the nature of things.

It is true that the division between the exoteric and esoteric is in need of some adjustment. It assumes that the texts can be clearly divided up. But this division cannot be made as clearly as I have said. To be exact, we have to say that the dividing line passes through both the *Scripta* and the seminars themselves. In each of the two groups we find the coexistence of propositions that qualify as protreptics and propositions that are doctrinal. The first, in contrast to Plato and Aristotle, are not in the dialogue form.[15] This is easily explained: the dialogue is a lost art, quite simply because, among moderns, every literary technique has become obsolete. Norden, in *Die antike Kunstprosa* (Leipzig: B. G. Teubner, 1898, 48), developed a theory according to which not a single ancient writing is an *atechnon*; the reciprocal is also true: every modern writing, at least insofar as it is modern, is an *atechnon*. This is what makes it the case that each is always unique in its genre. One finds in this the mark of the One for which there is no substitute, which is characteristic of the oeuvre form.

But Lacan is a modern. So he freely uses the powers of the *atechnon*, and of that for which there is no substitute. He is similar in this respect to André Breton, whose *Nadja* is the overlooked but nevertheless determining framework for every Lacanian writing. *Atechnon* reigns supreme, whether it be in his seminars, or his writings. Lacan was not only inclined to set aside the remaining bits of scholastic *technai* that the university tradition has left to us (parts, chapters, paragraphs distinct from sentences)—not at all out of ignorance, or out of contempt, but just because they were not pertinent. Even protreptics takes on, in his written paragraphs, the a-technical form of the scholarly conversation, as taken up by Macrobius, via La Mothe Le Vayer (cited for example in "Kant with Sade," Lacan 2006j, 664).[16] And since such a conversation can no longer occur in the dialogue form, the only thing left is a form that is not one: the *excursus*.[17]

In prose, in order to violently dislodge a sleeping *doxa* out of its resting place, negative protreptics no longer possesses the resources of taking people to task and diatribes. So, what we could readily call "Gongorist" proceedings appear instead. A minimal familiarity with Gongora suffices to show that the two are entirely different things. From the point of view of a history of styles, what we have instead is an *écriture artiste*, an art of writing that was kept alive in the hothouse environment of the hospital world since the time of the Goncourts, thanks to cultured doctors and lovers of beautiful things (Clérambault, du Boulbon).[18] But Lacan used it for other purposes; the rare lexeme, the unusual semanteme, and the roundabout syntax prevent the reader from relying on his or her linguistic habits, and make the reader suspicious of linear succession and symmetrical disposition, forcing him or her to guess at what will come.

Propositions that count as the transmission of knowledge are joined to the constant excursus, to the complex phrases that clear the way for knowledge. The latter are entirely different.[19] Their difference is glaringly obvious when Lacan uses mathematical writing for them. But well before the matheme properly so called, the transmissible proposition can be found—indicated by its syntax (as simple as possible) and its recurrence. It is useful to use the name *logion* for it, a term borrowed from the philology of the Gospels but for entirely secular purposes.

Because of the existence of the *logia* we can conclude that Lacan, a reader of Leo Strauss,[20] did not systematically practice the art of writing, and does not require the reading techniques that Leo Strauss tried to revive. This art and these techniques assume, in fact (1) that truly important propositions only appear in a complete form very few times in an oeuvre (and potentially never); (2) that as a general rule, frequently repeated propositions are not repeated without some variation—potentially minimal, but always revealing; (3) that propositions repeated identically (when there are any) are by that very fact to be considered inessential or fragmentary; (4) that the principal characteristic of propositions that are repeated (with or without variation) is usually their banality, their total inaccuracy with respect to the most obvious facts, if not their incoherence (these are traits that are supposed to arouse the reader's attention and justify a "second reading"); (5) that an oeuvre thus composed is for the most part a web of inessential, anodyne, and illogical propositions (and in this lies the enigma to be untangled); and (6) that in general every proposition of such an oeuvre, in order to be linked to what is important, coherent, and nontrivial, must be read as a fragment to be completed. This method consists of linking it to other propositions in the oeuvre, which are apparently barely compatible with it, if not contradictory, and are equally incomplete.[21]

None of this is true for the *logia*: they are repeated, veridical, essential, and able to be interpreted entirely on their own. They are neither anodyne, nor inconsistent, nor incomplete. They are not enigmatic.

If they appear so to a careless reader, it is because their affirmation is always in anticipation of a thought (an assertion of anticipated certitude). They are not shorthand for established thoughts, but rather holograms of thoughts to come; they are to be read in the future anterior. They are in and of themselves the source of their own light. They are made transparent by tireless repetition and by a repeated and quasi-material manipulation—Lacan himself engages in this work, whence their recurrence—and not by linking them to other propositions. The *logia* fall under the heading of the *bien dire*.

It is true that Lacan practiced in addition a "*mi-dire*" (see p. 109); this implies that certain propositions of knowledge can only be read as resections of the true, and in a fragmentary way; it also implies that other ones—they are sometimes the same—mix together elements of knowledge and protreptic procedures (digressions, *écriture artiste*). Thus neither of the two are *logia*, and in Lacan, nothing but *logia* count as knowledge. But the *mi-dire* is itself subordinated to *bien dire*. [22] The former is a way of access to the latter. Now, a *bien dire* (whether it be through a lapsus, a witticism, or felicitous wording) happens with a single roll of the dice. A *logion* only appears as the result of a good roll, but in the game of *logion*, one wins or loses by throwing the dice only once.[23]

It is true that the art of *bien dire* is difficult; perhaps it can only function as an ethical command (Lacan 1990a [1973], 22); perhaps *mi-dire* alone is prudent. In order for the gaming table to not be entirely empty sometimes the bets have to be split up, and one has to pretend that one is rediscovering Leo Strauss, who believes only in *mi-dire* and leaves the *logion* to God. Whence the more modest stakes, in which one can only win by betting multiple times.

Thus, in Lacan, sentences with different statuses—protreptic circumventions and propositions of knowledge—are intertwined. But their knotting together, being in itself a-technical, can only be unstable; it can thus only be read in the weakened form of juxtaposition (digression, detour, elusiveness). To anyone who is committed to knowledge, protreptics thus appears to be a connective tissue that interferes with the thread of transmissibility. To anyone who is committed to scholarly discussions, filled with ingenious aperçus, brilliant suggestions, masterful erudition, and an audacious style, the mathematized proposition seems opaque and skeletal. It is up to the reader to show some tact, just as Lacan advises the analyst, and not to conflate the different types of propositions.

This, then, is how we should understand the true relation between the *Scripta* and the seminars: the two sets contain propositions of knowledge and protreptic propositions, but as far as knowledge is concerned, there is nothing in the seminars that is not in the *Scripta*.[24] From the point of view of protreptics and scholarly discussions, there can be different things in the *Scripta* and in the seminars. If there is something in the second that is not found in the first, this belongs to the category of learned conversation, not knowledge; but the inverse is not true. In any case, whoever is interested in knowledge always has the right, but not the duty, to neglect the seminars.

Given this situation, we must conclude the following: if the *Scripta* are the oeuvre, and not the seminars, this means that Lacan relied on writing alone (and not transcriptions) for the transmission of his doctrine. What is just an empirical detail—Lacan's spoken word—counts for nothing. So we will definitively reject the idealizing constellation that is rooted in it: Presence, the Master, Disciples, Commemoration. In fact, the entire doctrine of the matheme is developed in order to oppose such things (see below, chapter 4). What kept the sacramental theater going was nothing but the mythologization of what was just a simple fact: that Lacan taught orally.

But who hasn't taught orally, ever since the university became the host institution for doctrines? It is true that Lacan spoke in a way that few of his contemporaries did. But the same could be said of many others. I will not be so cruel as to recall Alain's elegiac embellishments on the living word of Lagneau, or C. M. des Granges's on Brunetière's.[25] What is so surprising about the fact that some of the idiosyncrasies of speech are able to come across in transcriptions? And why should they be emphasized? In truth, the fact that Lacan delivered an oral teaching is something that conflates it with the work of a typical academic, from which it needs to be distinguished; Sartre in this respect is infinitely more surprising, having for such a long time held up the public transmission of his speech.

At best, one could agree that Lacan practiced a disjunction between the written and the spoken that academics are not supposed to engage in. Dumézil supposedly gave Foucault the following advice: "Do not write anything that has not been spoken; do not say anything that is not destined to be written." We can see an academic custom in this rule of bi-univocal projection (which many French academics deal with very poorly, due as much to agraphia as to graphomania, as much to aphasia as to logorrhea; this is one of their lesser weaknesses). Lacan, certainly, breaks it but, once again, not more and rather less than Sartre does.

In any case, nothing would be more inappropriate than to mention Plato. Whatever Plato thought of writing, and he was less univocal about it than is said, he belonged to a world in which writing was still problematic, at least regarding its relation to truth.[26] We see something entirely different with Lacan, who is entirely situated in a universe in which the relation of writing to truth is no longer problematic. It is true that he did re-problematize the relation—in Freudian psychoanalysis, the Truth speaks, it does not write—but his trajectory, from beginning to end, assumes precisely the opposite of what Plato assumes.

Of course, this does not mean that the written, as such, necessarily has to take place in the form of the book; we know that in this respect Lacan was, first by necessity, and then by choice, beyond the book; he shares this trait with some others: André Breton—*Nadja*, as we've said, is an oeuvre insofar as it is an *atechnon*. But is it a book?—or Jakobson. Like them, and in contrast to Freud, he makes the oeuvre appear in a place split between the long and the short form, between authorized addresses and more circumscribed ones. But this does not affect the point: to read Lacan is to read what is written, and especially the *Scripta*, by clearing away the obscurities that occur in them occasionally due to protreptic speech.

2

Science's Core Doctrine

1. Science and the Equation of Subjects

Lacan posits an equation: "the subject upon which we operate in psychoanalysis can only be the subject of science" ("Science and Truth," Lacan 2006m, 729). This *equation of subjects* contains three affirmations: (1) psychoanalysis operates on a subject (and not, for example, on an ego), (2) there is a subject of science, and (3) these two subjects are one and the same.

What the three affirmations have in common is that they speak of the *subject*. How this should be understood depends on what can be called the *axiom of the subject*:

There is a subject distinct from any form of empirical individuality.[1]

This existential axiom uses a term and a distinction that sound entirely similar to claims made in Kantian and post-Kantian metaphysics. Whether they are synonymous with them is a question that will, for the moment, be left open.

The third affirmation states the equation itself. It is supported by historical relationships, but is not based on them. The first affirmation is about analytic practice (the verb *to operate* indicates this); it is not at all trivial; validity is given to it by the authority of someone who is supposed to know what psychoanalysis is really about, and specifically with how Freud understood it. The second affirmation makes use of a concept that Lacan takes in a precise sense—the "subject of science." But this concept is only partially Lacanian. The definition of science that it appeals to does not come from Lacan—he explains himself on this point adequately. What really comes from Lacan is the affirmation that a specific form of the subject (the one whose existence is posited by the axiom of the subject) follows from this definition of science. Now this, properly speaking, is a hypothesis.

So we can, and must, think that the equation of subjects depends on this hypothesis, which from now on will be called *the hypothesis of the subject of science*.

Modern science, insofar as it is science and insofar as it is modern, shapes a mode of the subject's constitution.

The definition of the subject of science can be derived from this:

The subject of science is nothing but the name of the subject insofar as, by hypothesis, modern science shapes a mode of its constitution.

Notice that the equation of subjects says nothing about psychoanalysis as a *theory*. In particular, it does not at all affirm that psychoanalysis itself is a science. Lacan is explicit on this point: the fact that "its *praxis* implies no other subject than that of science" is "to be distinguished from the question of knowing whether psychoanalysis is a science (that is, whether its field is scientific)" (Lacan 2006m, 733). The word *praxis*, as we can see, is used explicitly. It compels us to invoke *theoria*, and in light of this it is noteworthy that Lacan does not say that the equation of subjects affects analysis as *theoria*. This does not mean that this equation is not a proposition belonging to *theoria*; it means that it is situated at the intersection of *praxis* and *theoria*. It could be said that it expresses a *theoria* in a nascent state, one that resulted from a series of reflections that began about *praxis*. From this we can conclude that all of the propositions contained in Lacanian *theoria* assume the equation of subjects, because they in turn assume that the reflections on *praxis* have been completed. The equation thus plays a seminal role.

This tells us how important it is that the equation not be empty. It only avoids being empty on one condition: that the hypothesis of the subject of science itself not be empty. This assumes two things: that the notion of science is the object of a sufficiently worked-out theory and, this theory being granted, that it can be linked to the constitution of a subject.

There is indeed a theory of science in Lacan. It is quite complete, and nontrivial.[2] In order to reconstruct its coherence, we can at first establish what it is not, and may begin with the difference between Freud and Lacan. Because Freud also has a theory of science. It is very limited, and if one asks why there is one at all, the answer is simple. It is due to what is commonly called Freud's scientism, which in his case is nothing other than a commitment to the ideal of science.[3] This ideal is sufficient to bring about the wish that psychoanalysis be a science. I do say *ideal of science*. In fact, it is a matter of an ideal point—external, or infinitely distant—toward which the straight lines of a plane extend, one that simultaneously belongs to all of them and is never encountered among them. But it is not an *ideal science* that would somehow "incarnate" the ideal of science, which is a strictly imaginary determination, and one that is necessary in order for representations to be possible.[4]

It is true that we always need representations; it is especially hard to see how one can avoid giving oneself a representation of what science *must* be, when someone was as wedded to the ideal of science as Freud was. This is what an ideal science is. Generally, it is attributed with the characteristics of a science that exists at one's own time; then the question becomes: "what must psychoanalysis be in order to be a science that conforms to the model?" From this moment on what were characteristics are transformed into criteria. And at the same time the path to another type of scientism opens up: not that of the ideal of science, but that of the ideal science. Freud gives in to this, taking the features of the ideal science from others who were in his opinion more qualified than he was. We'll mention Helmholtz, Mach, and Boltzmann here, just to name the most significant.[5]

It is true that a transverse theory of science is added to this, one that runs through the thread of Freud's texts: not only a theory of what a science must be, but an answer to the question "why is there science rather than no science at all?" But this theory remains scattered about, and it is not clear that Freud would ever have agreed to put it together, as he did with his theory of religion.

On the question "why science," Lacan just takes up Freud's aphorisms and summarizes them as follows: science is, at its birth, a sexual technique (see Lacan 1978 [1973], 151). But he proceeds with caution on this matter, just as he does in his answer to the question "why is there psychoanalysis rather than no psychoanalysis at all?" In any case, a complete doctrine on the question of origins is not to be found. The Lacanian theory of science focuses on something else.

Though faithful to Freud on the preceding point, Lacan distances himself from him on the issue of the ideal of science: he does not believe in it. To be exact, he does not believe in it *for psychoanalysis*. Contrary to what one might think, the founding equation requires this. With respect to the practice of psychoanalysis, science does not play the role of an ideal point—potentially extended to infinity; science is not external to psychoanalysis, strictly speaking; on the contrary, science internally structures its very material. If we stick to geometrical language, the field of psychoanalysis can be thought of as the plane created by the straight lines of its propositions (with a shift that can be calculated, we can recognize

Queneau's interpretation of Hilbert here); if science were external to this plane, science could not structure it in a regulative way. There would thus be no sense in asking under what conditions psychoanalysis would be a science. And so there would no longer be any sense in presenting some well-constituted science as a model that psychoanalysis should follow. In other words, there is no ideal of science for psychoanalysis: there is not an ideal science for it either. Psychoanalysis will find within itself the foundations of its own principles and methods.

To put it another way, psychoanalysis will find itself to be so secure that it will be able to question science. "What is a science that includes psychoanalysis?" Lacan asks in 1965 (in the synopsis for the annual journal of the EPHE, reprinted on the back of the 1973 French edition of *Seminar XI*).[6] This suggests that science itself could turn out to be the most consistent form of an activity that will be called *analysis*, which is found in all domains of knowledge, and, while remaining identical to itself, appears at one and the same time in diverse forms. Psychoanalysis could offer itself as an ideal point for this type of analysis, organizing the epistemological field and allowing for an orientation within it (whence the theme of the "Lacanian orientation"). Far from consenting to the ideal of science, psychoanalysis is tasked with constructing an ideal of analysis for science.

The *Cahiers pour l'Analyse*, in its time, tried to establish such a point, and merely added that Marxism could and should be organized according to analysis as well.[7] One can see why it aligned itself at one and the same time with both psychoanalysis and epistemology. Starting from the ideal of analysis, one easily ends up with an ideal analysis, whose mannequin the good little Lacanians set about dressing up: reshaping mathematics, logic, physics, biology, etc., so that they would fit into it. But this is hardly of any importance, except socially.

2. The Theory of the Modern

The first characteristic that one can attribute to the Lacanian theory of science is thus explained. It must bring out this singular connection in which science is essential to the existence of psychoanalysis and yet, for this very reason, does not stand before it as an ideal. The most suitable relation for this purpose is found in what sound like historical terms: the terms "succession" and "break." Koyré is also used as a support, read through the lens of the extremely historicizing Kojève.

For the purposes of clarity, we will take the liberty here of adopting the habits of geometricians, who reason in terms of axioms and theorems. Here are the most important ones:

Kojève's theorems

1. *There is a break between the ancient world and the modern universe.*
2. *This break is due to Christianity.*

Koyré's theorems:

1. *There is a break between ancient* epistèmè *and modern science.*
2. *Modern science is Galilean science, whose epitome is mathematized physics.*
3. *By mathematizing its object, Galilean science strips it of its sensible qualities.*

Lacan's hypothesis:

Koyré's theorems are a special case of Kojève's theorems.[8]

Lacan's lemmas:

1. *Insofar as it is distinguished from the ancient world, modern science is formed by Christianity.*
2. *Since the distinction between Christianity and the ancient world comes from Judaism, modern science consists of what is Judaic in Christianity.*[9]
3. *All that is modern is in sync with Galilean science and there is nothing modern except that which is in sync with Galilean science.*

The hypothesis of the subject is also treated according to this arrangement. It goes through Descartes. We know that Lacan tirelessly commented on and analyzed the Cartesian *cogito* (see especially "The Instance of the Letter," Lacan 2006f, 429–30; and "Science and Truth," Lacan 2006m, 733–35). This insistence is ultimately based on the thesis that Descartes is the first modern philosopher, as modern.

This proposition had certainly been advanced many times before, notably by Hegel. But we must be clear about what is meant by *modern*. In the strict sense that Lacan gives to this word (lemma 3), it can only mean this: Descartes reveals, by virtue of the internal organization of his oeuvre, what the birth of modern science forces upon thought. Now, the Cartesian edifice depends, critically, on the *cogito*. So, it must be the case that scientific thought needs that to which the *cogito* attests. The fact that the author of the *Meditations* is also the creator of analytic geometry and the author of a *Dioptrics* certainly counts as good evidence for this. And it must not be the case that these are merely contingent facts. They are supported by a set of propositions that express what we can call Lacan's *radical Cartesianism*:

> *If Descartes is the first modern philosopher, it is because of the* cogito;
> *Descartes invents the modern subject;*
> *Descartes invents the subject of science;*
> *The Freudian subject, insofar as Freudian psychoanalysis is intrinsically modern, could not be anything other than the Cartesian subject.*

Of course, this is not just a matter of chronological correlation: a discursive affiliation is implied as well. The argument goes as follows: mathematized physics eliminates all the qualities of beings (theorem 3); a theory of the subject that wishes to answer to such a physics must also strip the subject of all its qualities. This subject, constituted according to what characterizes science, is the subject of science (definition, p. 18). The qualitative markers of empirical individuality, whether psychic or somatic, do not apply to this subject; the qualitative properties of the soul do not apply to it either: this subject is neither mortal nor immortal, pure nor impure, just or unjust, sinner or saint, damned or saved; not even the formal properties that for such a long time were thought to be constitutive of subjectivity itself apply to it: it has neither Self, nor reflexivity, nor consciousness.

Such is precisely the being that the *cogito* makes emerge, at least if the order of reasons is taken seriously. In fact, at the very moment at which the *cogito* is declared to be certain, it is disjoined, by hypothesis, from any quality—qualities being, from then on, collectively and individually subject to doubt. The very thought by which the *cogito* is defined is strictly nondescript; it is the minimum common to any possible thought, since any thought, whatever it may be (true or false, empirical or not, reasonable or absurd, affirmed, or denied, or put into doubt), can give me the opportunity to conclude that I am.

A correlate without qualities assumed by a thought without qualities: we can see how this being—called the subject by Lacan, but not by Descartes—corresponds to what modern science does.

True, Descartes does not stop here; he moves on without delay, as if in haste, to consciousness and to a thinking with qualities. Once he presents the following synonyms, we are certainly dealing with a thinking with qualities: "But then what am I? A thing that thinks. What is that? A thing that doubts, understands, affirms, denies, wills, refuses, and which also imagines and senses" (Descartes 1998 [1641], 63). We can then see why Lacan only signs on to what we can call the extreme point of the *cogito*, and why he makes every effort to stop the movement from the first moment to the second. This is why he limits the *cogito* to its enunciation alone, and why he, moreover, loops this enunciation back onto itself, making the conclusion ("therefore, I am") into the pure *pronuntiatum* of the premise ("I think"): "to write: *I think: 'therefore I am,'* with quotation marks around the second clause" ("Science and Truth," Lacan 2006m, 734). This ensures that a thought without qualities persists, ceasing just before it differentiates itself into doubt, conception, affirmation, negation, etc.[10]

But a thought without qualities is not appropriate only to modern science. Lacan demonstrates that it is also necessary for the foundation of the Freudian unconscious. The linchpin of Freud's program is found in an observation that we are forced to make due to a fact about dreaming (*factum somnii*): that there is thinking in dreams. Whence the line of reasoning: if there is thinking in dreams (and in witticisms, the parapraxes of everyday life, etc.), then thinking is not what the philosophical tradition says it is. In particular, it is not correlated to self-consciousness. But there is thinking in dreams (and in witticisms, the parapraxes of everyday life, etc.; this is what the *Traumdeutung* establishes, as well as later works); therefore, etc . . .

If we allow the name *unconscious* to stand for the negative proposition "self-consciousness is not a property essential to thinking," then we get the theorem:

If there is a thinking in the dream, there is an unconscious.

And we get at the same time the lemma:

The dream is the royal road to the unconscious.

And a definition that derives from the theorem and the lemma:

To affirm that there is an unconscious is equivalent to affirming that it thinks.[11]

Lacan just adds to this the proposition, which is drawn from Descartes and expanded to include Freud:

If there is thought, there is a subject.

This reasoning, however, is only true on two conditions. First of all, it must be possible for there to be a subject even where there is neither consciousness nor self—this requires a nontrivial theory of the subject; secondly, the thinking that is the stuff of dreams and botched actions must be able to be disjoined from any quality. In this way the phenomena are saved.[12]

According to Lacan, Freudianism is based on these three affirmations: that there is an unconscious, that the unconscious is no stranger to thinking, and that it is also therefore no stranger to the subject of thinking. If it were, psychoanalysis would be illegitimate in principle and no doubt impossible as a practice. In fact, an unconscious foreign to the subject who thinks would be somatic, and the somatic has nothing to do with either truth or speech; psychoanalysis, of course, deals with truth and speech. The unconscious, insofar as psychoanalysis deals with it, is thus no stranger to either the subject or thinking. So, neither the subject nor thinking requires consciousness.

But to say that self-consciousness is not a constitutive property of the subject is to offer a rebuttal to the philosophical tradition, especially Descartes. We mean the second Descartes, the one as eager to leave the extreme point of the *cogito* as prisoners are to escape from prison. After Freud, self-consciousness becomes just one aspect of empirical individuality, one that philosophy unduly introduced into the subject, however meticulously filtered through its needs that it was. Psychoanalysis thus takes the axiom of the subject more strictly than any other doctrine does. With unrivaled precision it separates out two beings: in one, self-consciousness can without contradiction be taken to be inessential; in the other, self-consciousness cannot without contradiction be taken to be inessential. Only the first answers exactly to the call of science, and it alone falls within the limits fixed by the axiom of the subject; it will thus be called, completely legitimately, the subject of science. And we can now understand why it is the Cartesian just as much as it is the Freudian subject.[13] As for the second being, the name *ego* is as good for it as any other.

The theory of science is derived from Koyré and Kojève, the interpretation of Descartes as both a scholar and metaphysician is based on Koyré, the interpretation of the *cogito* depends upon Gueroult, the axiom of the subject goes back, homonymously and synonymously, to the post-Kantian tradition . . . but the hypothesis of the subject of science, the equation of subjects, the interpretation of Freud entailed by it, and the combination of them all is specific to Lacan. This is why it is appropriate to speak in Lacan's case not so much of a theory of science, nor even of an epistemology, but of an actual *Core Doctrine of science*. By this we mean specifically the conjunction of propositions on science and propositions on the subject.

3. The Historicist Style

At first sight, every aspect of science's Core Doctrine is fundamentally historicizing: the hypothesis of the subject of science ("a certain moment of the subject that I consider to be an essential correlate of science, a historically defined moment . . . , the moment Descartes inaugurates that goes by the name of *cogito*" ["Science and Truth," Lacan 2006m, 727]); the hypothesis concerning science ("the decisive change that, with physics paving the way, founded *Science* in the modern sense" [ibid., 727]); and the articulation of science to the subject ("in this situation, what seems radical to me is the modification that has occurred in our subject position, in the sense that it is inaugural therein and that science continues to strengthen it ever further. Koyré is my guide here" [726–27]).

The historicism intensifies the more closely Koyré is followed. Based on his own theorems, Koyré derived two distinguishing features that, according to him, make Galilean science distinct from any other group of discourses that would claim to be a science. The first one is:

A Galilean science combines two traits: empiricism and mathematization.

True, this first distinguishing feature could be interpreted in nonhistorical terms. All that would be needed is a general interpretation of the term "empiricity" and an answer to the question "how do we recognize that a proposition is empirical?" But Koyré himself says nothing of the sort. In an effort to shed more light on the first distinguishing feature, he completes it with a second that is just as historicizing:

Granted that any empirical being can be handled technologically, and that mathematization is the paradigm of any theory, Galilean science is a theory of technology, and technology is the practical application of science.

The value of this distinguishing feature apparently consists entirely in its ability to describe and exhaustively explain what we can all see happening today: "the galloping form of its [i.e., science's] interference in our world," "the chain reactions that characterize what one might call the expansions of its energetics" ("Science and Truth," Lacan 2006m, 726). Lacan takes the lunar expeditions to be evidence of this: "the ALM landing on the moon, or Newton's formula realized in a machine" ("Radiophonie," Lacan 2001d [1970], 423; see equally *Television*, Lacan 1990a [1973], 36). Now, these are the kinds of proofs that a historian of the present uses, just as the first distinguishing feature is in fact supported by the kinds of proofs a historian of the past would use.

A few consequences can be drawn from the first distinguishing feature: science's object is the totality of what exists empirically—we can call this the universe—and it treats it with as much precision as the disciplines of letters treat their object. In other words, literalized science is, as such, a precise science.[14] Now, this can also be interpreted in historical terms.

Consider Galileo's aphorism: "[the great book of the universe] is written in the language of mathematics, and its characters are triangles, circles, and other geometrical figures" (Galileo 1960 [1623], 184). This can only be understood completely if we take humanism into consideration (Florence was for a long time its capital, and Galileo was Tuscan). To speak of the book of Nature or the world or the universe is in itself an ancient trope, but it takes on a new significance once scholars started using printed volumes, and after the editing of texts received strict rules. To speak of the characters of such a book is to go back to Democritus, Epicurus, and Lucretius (Redondi has noted the perhaps crucial importance of this affiliation),[15] but it is also to say something different after typography itself was subjected to geometrical forms, and after corrections turned out to depend occasionally on the shape of a letter.

In other words, literality, which is at one and the same time its index and means, sheds light on how far mathematization can go when it comes to Nature; but it immediately develops into something more: a demand for precision. Thanks to humanism, all of the disciplines of the letter (let's say: philology) are the ideal science as far as precision is concerned. The physicist must be as precise with respect to the universe (and as free from inherited biases) as Estienne was with respect to Plato's *text*, as Laurent Valla was with respect to the *text* of Constantine's Donation, or as Erasmus was with the *text* of the Evangelists. . . . such is what the very word *book* requires.

This means that the apparently direct move from literality to precision can only be fully explained by history. The same is true for the apparently direct move from precision to instrumentation. For Galileo, mathematics and measurement were the ways—just some of the ways, it would turn out—that would allow mere physics to one day acquire the status that mighty philology had already had for a long time as far as the science of language (grammar) and the science of written documents were concerned. It is true that precision with respect to empirical material requires instruments that are themselves material—ones quite different from those that philology uses and which were, without a doubt, for Galileo, quite inferior in dignity. Modern science, insofar as it is empirical, is not only experimental: it is instrumental.[16]

This is where the second distinguishing feature comes in. It has always been the case that technology is the material treatment, by material instruments, of empirical material; once science takes the empirical as its object, technology can and must provide it with the instruments it needs; since ultimately the science that takes the empirical as its object is also a literal[17] science, that is, a precise science, the instruments supplied by technology can and must be made into precision instruments. It just so happens that technological progress at the time allowed for this, thanks to the great engineers of the Renaissance: once again, this is a historical thesis.

The universe of modern science is at one and the same time a universe of precision and a universe of technology. But science is only literally precise if the instruments produced by technology materially allow it to be. It is true that for Galileo they only allow for precision to the extent that science presides over their conception and their execution. Such is the true meaning of the telescope and of his relation to engineers. This is how the modern universe is configured: a union of science and technology so close and reciprocal that one can just as well say that we are dealing with the same thing in two forms, that there is just one science that is sometimes fundamental and sometimes applied, or else that there is just one technology that is sometimes theoretical and sometimes practical.[18]

4. Ancient *Epistèmè*

The historicism intensifies again when we consider how important the reference to antiquity is. It is vital. If science becomes a theory of technology, and technology becomes the practical application of science (see the second distinguishing feature), it is assumed that the couple theory/practice is an exact duplicate of the couple science/technology. In order to understand the distinctive significance of this overlap, we have to assume that it is not self-evident. The simplest way to be assured of this consists in establishing that it has not always been true, either because of geographical variation (this is the question about Chinese science) or temporal variation.

Koyré chose the second couple. In the ancient world, he finds that the couple *theoria/praxis* was entirely independent of the couple *epistèmè/ techne*. But this means that what appears to be a paradox in the former world can be resolved by moderns: an *epistèmè* existed, and many *technai* existed, alongside the nonexistence of productive machines. Koyré's doctrine thus ends with hypotheses about questions in the ancient world that are properly historical: about slavery, mechanization, labor.[19]

This is not an expansion that Koyré could have avoided. It seems to affect the hard kernel of his theorems, as he himself formulates them. Taken in their original form these are, we have seen, fundamentally differentiating. They speak of Galilean science, but the distinctive traits that they attribute to it are only fully grasped in a relation of opposition and difference. But the two opposing and differential terms are put in historical language. In fact, the opposition between antiquity and modern times is the linchpin of what we call history, while many hold the opposite: that we can only speak of antiquity and modernity if we allow for history. Galilean science can only be understood completely if we understand what it is not, but in Koyré's theory what it is not can only be approached in historical terms. Koyré is not only historicizing, which after all could just be a matter of style; he is a historian.

Epistèmè turns out to be complete only when it has revealed what it is that makes any object unable to be otherwise than it is, necessarily and for all time. More precisely still, what makes a discourse into an *epistèmè* is just the totality of what this discourse takes to be eternal and necessary about its object. From this it follows that an object lends itself all the more naturally to *epistèmè* the more easily the latter can demonstrate what it is in the object that makes it eternal and necessary, so that there is no science of what can be otherwise than it is, and the most complete science is the science of the most eternal and most necessary object. From this it also follows that humanity can only do science because of what binds humanity to the eternal and the necessary; there is a name for this: it is *the soul*. It is distinguished from the body, which is what links humanity to the fleeting and contingent. From this it follows, finally, that mathematics is the paradigm of choice for science.

Because the mathematics inherited from the Greeks deals with the necessary and the eternal, Figures and Numbers cannot be otherwise than they are, and at the same time they cannot come into being or cease to be—they are as they are, for all eternity. The necessity we get from demonstrations is only valid to the exact extent to which it is co-natural to necessity in itself. Just as the trajectories of celestial bodies crystallize for our bodily eyes the most adequate figure of the eternal, similarly the path that goes from principles and axioms to conclusions crystallizes for the eyes of the soul the most adequate figure of the necessary.

Inversely, the empirical in all its diversity does not cease coming into being or ceasing to be. So it is incessantly otherwise than it is. It is thus intrinsically alien to mathematics. If, however, mathematics is able to grasp anything at all in the realm of the diverse, then it will be what lets itself be seen as identical to itself and eternal: the Same as such. Let's say that certain objects available to the senses that can be completely mathematized are assumed to be eternal beings in themselves—such as celestial bodies, or harmonies. Or that certain senses emanate more directly from the soul than others—like the gaze.[20] Or that one can and must extract some glimmer of the eternal from every object that is available to any of the senses. If it is appropriate to call this glimmer contained in each being the Idea, one can see why some ancients defined Ideas by Numbers and why Numbers were just one way to access the Same. This is why they were important, and not because of the calculations that they eventually made possible.

This is especially the case since Number is not the only mark of the Same. Even more fundamental was the necessity we get from demonstrations. Greek *epistèmè* is founded on them and them alone; mathematicity is only a secondary result. The radical and definitive move consists of drawing conclusions from guaranteed principles and self-evident axioms; conclusions that conform to the rules of reason while respecting phenomenal appearances at the same time. Now, mathematics offers the purest type of demonstration, even if a specific discipline, like logic or dialectics, is needed in order to bring forth its rules: (a) the principle of the object's uniqueness and the domain's homogeneity: all the propositions of science must concern elements of one and the same domain and must relate to a unique object; (b) the principle of the minimum and the maximum: the propositions of science are either theorems or axioms, and a maximal number of theorems must be able to be deduced from a minimal number of axioms, expressed by a minimal number of basic concepts; and (c) the principle of evidence: all the axioms and basic concepts must be self-evident, which means that one does not have to demonstrate and define them.[21]

Mathematics reigns supreme because it offers the purest type of demonstration; it offers this because the beings that it deals with, numbers or figures, are as close as possible to the eternal and the perfect. Nothing from the sensible realm is able to alter the necessity of its *logoi*. Mathematics is thus the formal paradigm of *epistèmè* as such—of that which in any particular *epistèmè* makes it an *epistèmè* in itself, and of that which in any discourse makes it into a particular *epistèmè* (whence the usefulness of the *more geometrico*: in order to show, beyond even mathematics, how *epistèmè* is articulated).

At the same time, we can see why mathematics is this formal paradigm to the precise extent that it *is not* the supreme *epistèmè* itself. It is not the supreme *epistèmè* because its object is not the supreme object; but it serves as a model because its object, stripped as much as possible of sensible substance, resembles the supreme object as much as it is possible to, thanks to its formal properties. If what makes a discourse scientific is due to what this discourse grasps regarding what is eternal, perfect, and necessary in its object, and if moreover there exists an object about which one can say that it is the most necessary, the most perfect, and the most eternal, because in fact it is nothing if not the necessary, the perfect, and the eternal in itself . . . then the only full and complete science is one that, conforming to the mathematical paradigm, is directed toward this object, which is above and beyond any mathematics: namely, God, if this is the appropriate name for the necessary, perfect, and eternal being. Number can give access to it, the best access, even the only one perhaps, but Number is not God. Mathematics alludes to what it is not, at the very moment when its reign is established, but this allusion is supposed to redirect our gaze toward a supreme Being.

At the same time, the very possibility of science among humanity arises from what links us to the necessary and the eternal. The name for this link, as we've said, is *the soul*, whether this is taken to be a localizable region in human beings, or a quasi-geometrical space that contains the points where the link is made. As for *the body*, which is what marks humanity with the contingent and the transitory, it sometimes alludes to something else and it is sometimes an obstacle: it alludes to something else with those of its parts that most resemble, in their materiality, material beings that themselves allude to the necessary and the eternal (the gaze, which resembles light; proportional beauty, which alludes to calculable symmetries); it is an obstacle in every other respect. Because of this, a filter is needed in order to get rid of the impurities that come from the body; purifying techniques play this role. Thus, an *epistèmè* is only achieved for a being endowed with a soul and a body who has also submitted both to the appropriate exercises.

Having arrived at the end of these exercises, the scholar will recognize the fact that logical necessity in science is nothing but the mark that the necessity of the being of each being imprints on discourse. Aristotle does not at all contradict Plato on this point. When he defines the syllogism—this was, as we know, the general name for reasoning before it became the technical name for a particular form of it—he says it is "a discourse in which, certain things being posited, a different thing . . . results necessarily" (*ex anankes*). But this repeats the *Timaeus*, which connects regulated thought to the discourse of celestial bodies: "God invented and gave us sight to the end that we might behold the courses of intelligence in the heavens, and apply them to the courses of our own intelligence which are akin to them, the unperturbed to the perturbed; and that we, learning them and partaking of the natural truth of reason, might imitate the absolutely unerring courses of God and regulate our own vagaries" (*Timaeus*, 47b).[22] The Academy and the Lyceum both attest to ancient *epistèmè*'s internal tendency, such as it is understood in Koyré's theorem and in science's Core Doctrine. The necessity contained in the *logoi*, as necessity, is the point in science where the resemblance between the necessary being of being and the necessary being of the knower is at its fullest: conversely, science is nothing if it is not the attainment of this resemblance which, thanks to the purified soul, unites human beings endowed with bodies to the incorporeal supreme Being: there is no science except of the necessary. More generally still than the envelopment of the microcosm by the macrocosm (however frequent this imaginary schema is), the prime mover of knowledge is the pursuit of resemblance all the way up to the necessary.

The Galilean event is clarified by way of contrast: first, mathematics, in science, can cover *all* of the empirical realm, without regard to any hierarchy of being, and without ordering objects on a scale going from the less perfect (which is intrinsically alien to Number) to the more perfect (which is entirely numerable); second, mathematics, covering all of the empirical realm, has a role to play because of its literality, that is, due to calculation rather than demonstration (the emergence of science also means the inexorable decline of the *mos geometricus*); and third, mathematics covers the empirical realm *as such*, including what is transitory, imperfect, and opaque about it.

So we can see why science is connected to technology.[23] Not that the ancient world had no technology. But, if one believes science's Core Doctrine on this point, it did not link technology in any privileged way to *epistèmè*. More exactly, there are two pairs available: *techne/epistèmè, theoria/ praxis*. The modern universe superimposes them. Of course, then their wording becomes straightaway illegitimate. In the ancient world there is no reason for the pairs to coincide with each other. If they do coincide, they can only be intertwined in such a way that an ancient word appears able to unify traits that today we would say are incompatible. This means that, in the Greek system, there is a share of *theoria* in *techne* and a share of *praxis* in *epistèmè*. Of course, this is why Socrates interrogates artisans, in order to get them to extract, by a sort of filtering procedure, the kernel of the *theoria* that they possess; and this is certainly why those who possess *epistèmè* must also act purely—science is connected to consciousness [*conscience*], which is what governs its actions (*praxeis*).

The modern break thus requires that mathematics, to some extent, cease to be partially linked to the eternal. Mathematizable beings (and especially celestial bodies) are no longer *as such* assumed to be eternal or perfect: one could still think that they are, but this would be for other reasons, and if one in fact must stop thinking that they are (if one discovers sunspots, for example), this certainly does not affect the possibility of mathematizing their trajectory. In the same way, it could still be the case that the necessity of mathematical demonstrations is taken to display the necessity of Being, but this is no longer due to divine analogy, and moreover, it will not describe the way science makes use of these demonstrations.

In this case numbers no longer function as Numbers, the golden key to the Same, but as letters and, as letters, they must grasp what is ceaselessly other in the realm of the diverse. The empirical realm is able to be rendered into letters [*littéralisable*] insofar as it is empirical; letters do not carry the object off toward the heaven of Ideas; heaven is not the visible unfolding of the infinite sphere of Being; rendering into letters [*littéralisation*] is not idealization.

The event thus does not consist of the fact that modern science becomes mathematical; ancient science already was and, in certain respects, modern science is even less so. Rather than mathematical, modern science should in fact be called *mathematized*. Numbers, as letters, and thus calculation, come first in mathematization—not the good logical form of demonstrations. For the Greeks, science is mathematics; the mathematicity of number, insofar as it permits counting, does not play a role in it, but what makes it the case that Number gives access to the Same in itself does; let's say, the *logos*, as necessary demonstration.

Now, taking a detour through *epistèmè* is not only important for Koyré. It is also one of the most important moments in the Lacanian arrangement. If Lacan in part connects psychoanalysis to the emergence of the modern universe, this becomes, quite obviously, one of its positive conditions.

But science's Core Doctrine says more: psychoanalysis also has a negative condition: the disappearance of ancient science. In other words, there is something in *epistèmè* that is so radically connected to psychoanalysis that it is able to prevent its emergence: to understand *epistèmè* is thus also to understand psychoanalysis, not only by way of contrast, but due to an intimate mutually exclusive relationship.

But if *epistèmè* is nothing more than a historical figure, then our understanding of psychoanalysis is radically historicist. But history, according to Lacan himself, is fallacious. Is it then necessary to conclude that science's Core Doctrine, such as it unfolded, is fallacious? That the hypothesis of the subject of science, which connects psychoanalysis to modern science, is just an appearance to be destroyed? That it is at best a way to make things understood, but one that must be rejected as soon as it has been used: "throw my book away," as Gide said; or "the ladder must be thrown away after climbing it," as Wittgenstein said? Is this the Core Doctrine's last word?

5. Historicism Is Not Necessary

I do not, however, think this is an inevitable result, and the figure of *epistèmè* itself provides us with the best proof. The persistence of its relevance for psychoanalysis is not a matter of remembrance, but of the present.

More exactly, it is due to a logic. We've described *epistèmè*'s form: it has distinctive characteristics, and these have been supported by archival references. But, as convenient and even as precise as they are, [24] they are mere ballast and not at all essential. It suffices that the form be consistent, and that it answers to whatever discourses are developed. It is not necessary that, in fact, the period referred to as antiquity was familiar with this form only, nor is it necessary that this form only be attested to during this period. If someone were to demonstrate the existence of a discourse in Greece or Rome that was simultaneously mathematized and empirical, it would certainly weaken Koyré's position;[25] it would not necessarily weaken science's Core Doctrine. And if someone were to demonstrate the existence, in the modern universe, of a discourse conforming to the rules of *epistèmè*, this would not weaken Koyré's theorems at all.

The same reasoning holds, moreover, for geographical matters: it does seem to be the case that outside of the West there is no discourse to be found that conforms to science's Core Doctrine. But it is not essential to Lacan that this be the case. In fact, in the arrangement Lacan adheres to, the *epistèmè* from which modern science separates itself is more a structural form than a properly historical entity. It is characterized by a totality of theses, not dates, even if a natural relationship between the theses and the dates could be established. The theses that define it rely on the status of mathematics and on how the transitory realm of contingency relates to the realm of eternal necessity.

The power of these theses has not disappeared entirely. At the most basic level, who would doubt that traits of Euclidean demonstration can still be found in the forms of the ideal science? Many recent discourses openly adhere to an epistemology of the minimum and maximum, which has no other source but a Greek one. As we shall see, this is one of the paradoxical traits of structuralisms. If the soul is, as Lacan thinks, basing himself on science's Core Doctrine, intimately correlated to *epistèmè* and its constitutive principles, who would deny that the soul is still a recurrent feature in the most mundane statements we make? Couldn't we even say that the current discourse of civilized democracy finds its most solid footing in the soul? Contrary to what we often believe, we find not the Judeo-Christian (a progressive variant of the Judeo-Masonic) holding sway over our religions, spiritualisms, humanitarian gestures, and political Tartufferie, but that of the Same coming from the ancients. The fact that the demiurge of the *Timaeus* and Aristotle's prime mover have been reduced to the status of Santa Claus, assumed to be able to fix anything visibly wrong that appears to the eyes of the body by a gain visible only to the eyes of the soul . . . this can make us either laugh or cry, but it is not incomprehensible.

As for science, as proud as it is of its modernity: is not the most insistent demand addressed to it that it enlighten people's consciences? It is still widely believed that a great scholar should be a moral authority. On the condition that what he says is just a repetition of what everyone already thinks spontaneously, at least when they do think: this is what is called, in a word that also comes from the Greeks, ethics. I will not question whether any ethics is legitimate in the modern universe.[26] One thing is certain, however: if ethics exists, science has nothing to say about it and, without a doubt, as science, it has nothing to do with it.

Certainly we can still reason along historicist lines; we can go back to the language of Gramsci and say that modern man is never contemporary with himself (he is a "walking anachronism," he wrote in his prison [Gramsci 1971, 324 note II]). But Lacan is more radical: that is, more Freudian.

In a well-known passage from his *Introduction to Psychoanalysis*, Freud mentions three "major blows" that "the *naive* self-love of men has had to submit to . . . at the hands of science" (Freud 1963 [1917], 284–85).

Copernicus, by calling geocentrism into question; Darwin and Wallace with natural selection; and psychoanalysis. This is how he explains the excessive hostility the latter suffers from, which is comparable in his eyes to the rage endured by his great predecessors. It hardly matters after all if he was right about the historical details (Lacan, for his part, doubted it, privileging Kepler over Copernicus). Beyond these details, we should focus on a fundamental thesis: there is a recurrent anti-Copernicanism, and it is connected to the Ego.

The term that Freud uses, *Eigenliebe* [self-love], certainly has a moral connotation (one thinks of *amor sui*, as well as the *amour-propre* of the *Maximes*), but this can be removed from the term and we can boil it down to its material kernel, which is the Ego.[27] Now, the Ego is a structure, and it is a structure because it is just the name for an imaginary function. This is what is affected by modern cosmology, regardless of whether it is attributed to Copernicus or Kepler. What is important about the former's heliocentrism is not so much that it demotes the position of the Earth, but that it establishes a radical disharmony between the geometrical center of the planetary system and the center of observation, which remains where humanity is located: the step taken by Kepler promotes, over the circle, an ellipse with two focal points, one of which is forever empty. In both cases the circle's good form, in which every focal point coincides with every focal point, is replaced by a bad form.[28]

Setting itself against this, anti-Copernicanism is structurally unavoidable because the Ego and the imaginary, by their very laws, privilege good forms. It is thus true that *epistèmè* as a historical figure has disappeared, but some of its characteristic traits remain because the Ego remains, regardless of the period.

Whence the following propositions, which can be drawn from both Freud and Lacan:

> *The Ego hates science;*
> *The Ego hates letters as such;*
> *The Ego and the imaginary are Gestaltist;*
> *Science and letters are indifferent to good forms;*
> *The imaginary as such is radically foreign to modern science;*
> *Modern science, insofar as it is literal, dissolves the imaginary.*

On this basis the vocabulary of periodization, when it appears in Lacan, can be better assessed and, since it is so close to Kojève's neo-Hegelian style, the vocabulary of broad generalizations as well. Thanks to these two vocabularies, clever people have not had any trouble giving one of the possible responses to the question of knowing why Lacan needed a theory of science. It was not, they say, because of scientism, since Lacan did not believe in the ideal of science for psychoanalysis, and even less in the ideal science. Instead, it was because of his historicizing theses: "the emergence of Galilean science made psychoanalysis possible," or "psychoanalysis is not conceived without the suturing that modern science brings about with respect to the subject (to which the *Cogito* attests)," or "psychoanalysis could only emerge in the infinite universe of science," etc. The problem is that these responses in themselves do not mean anything; they only repeat the question in another form.

More generally speaking, we must not get too taken in by Lacan's broad generalizations; this is a Lacan of scholarly conversation and protreptics, but not a Lacan of knowledge.

As it happens, periodization has a very specific role to play: it destroys the applicability of the couple *ideal of science/ideal science* to psychoanalysis. What could do this better than the operators of succession and break, for which relativism and its highbrow companion, nominalism, come so easily? I will dare to advance the following: Freud, in a period that was dominated by philosophical idealism, had to rely on the scientism of the ideal of science in order to clear the way for psychoanalysis; the price to pay for this was nothing less than the ideal science's scientism. Lacan, at a time when psychoanalytic institutions were dominated by the ideal science's scientism, had to relativize and nominalize in order to clear the way for psychoanalysis; the price to pay for this was a periodizing discourse. In both cases, it was a matter of accomplishing a similar goal by different means. In both cases, this was done with protreptics. Now, if we want to access the hard kernel of knowledge, we need to make it logically independent of protreptics. As it happens, this is also to make it independent of successions and chronological simultaneities.

So we are just following Lacan here, who did everything he could to reduce the costs and disengage from historical narratives. From the moment that the periodizing language accomplished its goal, from the moment that, thanks to it, the double illusion *ideal science/ideal of science* became powerless, Lacan immediately set out to eliminate the theory of breaks. This is what discourse theory is meant to do, which he developed starting in 1969;[29] its purpose was to extract the properties of discourse in general (let's recall that discourse, for Lacan, is a social bond) and, by doing so, to demonstrate that heterogeneity and multiplicity are intrinsic to it. They are not simply the effects, in discourse, of periods and epochs that would otherwise be extrinsic to discourses. And they especially cannot simply be taken in terms of successions ("this is not in any sense to be viewed as a series of historical emergences" [*Seminar XX*, Lacan 1998 (1975), 16]). With a doctrine on the plurality of places, the plurality of terms, on the differences between the properties of places and the properties of terms, on the changeability of terms relative to places, we get what we could call a non-chronological articulation and, more broadly, a non-successive concept of breaks. No doubt the emergence of a new discourse, the passage from one discourse to another (what Lacan calls the "quarter turn" ["Allocution sur l'enseignement," Lacan 2001d (1970), 300])—change, in other words—can constitute an event; no doubt such events are objects that historians try to grasp chronologically. But they are not what the historians say they are. Every history, in this respect, ends up being fallacious, and the first mistake is found precisely in the minimal amount of homogenization presupposed by any temporal series. In itself, the quarter turn does not have to be part of a chronological series.

Granted that discourse theory renders places and terms into letters, a break is then primarily the hallmark of an impossibility associated with the literal. It is impossible that one system of letters be another; it is impossible for a system of letters to change, without disruptions, into another system of letters. In other words, there is no such thing as an internal transformation of a system; every transformation is a passage from one system to another.

More profoundly, we can hold that a discourse defined this way is in itself just a set of rules for determining synonyms and non-synonyms. Two discourses will be different from each other to the exact extent that their defining rules are themselves different. The nature of a discursive break can thus be put this way:

> *To say that there is a break between two discourses is just to say that none of the propositions of one are synonymous with any of the propositions of the other.*

From this we can conclude that there can only be synonyms—if any exist—within one and the same discourse, and that between different discourses the only possible resemblances are actually homonyms. In such a theory, the concepts of break and discourse thus completely go together: between two truly different discourses the only relationship there can be is that of a break, and "break" is just the name for their real difference. So the following conclusion imposes itself on us:

A break is fundamentally not chronological.

The same thing can be said differently, expanding its scope:

Discourse theory is an anti-history.

From this comes the fact that here synchrony does not mean contemporaneity. Instead, synchrony must be understood in the same sense in which we can say that two pendulums are synchronous. We can easily understand how, among statements from the same date, or in the heart of one and the same statement, there may be non-synchrony. Likewise, the passage from one discourse to another need not lead to univocal successions; statements synchronous to *epistèmè* can succeed, in time, those of science, and conversely. More profoundly, the non-chronological doctrine of the break implies that succession is never anything but imaginary. There is no real ultimate authority that legitimates a series of orders.

The historicizing reading of science's Core Doctrine is only necessary if one limits oneself to the goals of protreptics: it is radically insufficient if the construction of knowledge is what is valued. So it is appropriate to state more explicitly the structural and intrinsic traits of Galilean science and not limit oneself to the chronicles of Galileo and his successors. Furthermore, this brings us back to a concern that Koyré himself had, who advanced some theses on this point. Lacan made use of these and, without always being entirely explicit about it, he developed others that completed them.

6. Literality and Contingency

It is possible to read Koyré without the historicizing operators. More exactly, it is possible to remove them from the reading that Lacan's Core Doctrine proposes.

By combining mathematicity and the empirical, by uniting *theoria* and *praxis, epistèmè* and *techne,* Koyré's distinguishing features perform multiple operations. They can, however, be reduced to one. To understand it, it suffices to use an epistemology that is apparently quite distant from Koyré's: Popper's. Popper says that a scientific proposition must be able to be refuted, thus creating, under the name "demarcation," what we can also call *Popper's distinguishing feature*. Now, a proposition is only able to be refuted if its negation is not logically contradictory or materially invalidated by simple observation. In other words, its referent must be able—logically or materially—to be otherwise than it is. But this is what contingency is. In short, only a contingent proposition can be refuted; there is thus only a science of the contingent.

Reciprocally, anything that is contingent must be able to be grasped by science—theoretical as well as applied. The set of contingencies insofar as they are grasped by science, in theory and in practice, is the universe.

Such is the arrangement to which Lacan really belongs. Its middle term is the contingent, and this allows for a combination of Koyré's chronological distinguishing feature and Popper's structural distinguishing feature.[30] Science's Core Doctrine turns out to rest on a hidden lemma:

> *Koyré's distinguishing feature and Popper's distinguishing feature are synonyms, provided they are understood in terms of the contingent.*

A first consequence imposes itself on us: regardless of how it was formulated originally, Koyré's theorem is not fundamentally a historical proposition; if psychoanalysis depends on it, this is not due to historical reasons (and especially not to chronological reasons).

A second, more profound, consequence posits that the equation of the subjects be rewritten as follows:

> *The subject on which psychoanalysis operates, being a correlate of modern science, is a correlate of the contingent.*

In this rewriting, it turns out that Popper is necessary to Lacan. It is true that Lacan hardly ever refers to him (he does become interested in him belatedly, but without passion); however, it is indeed the word *contingent* that Lacan seizes on in Kojève and Koyré, who do not exactly use it : "the starry vault no longer exists, and the set of celestial bodies . . . present themselves as though they could just as well not be there—their reality is essentially marked . . . by a character of facticity, they are fundamentally contingent" (*Seminar VII*, Lacan 1992 [1986], 122). In the line of reasoning that goes from Koyré and Kojève's propositions to this promotion of contingency, we can restore the missing link, despite Lacan's ignorance of Popper, and Popper's of Lacan.

If, however, we were to stick to what Lacan might have explicitly thought, is it illegitimate to evoke Mallarmé here? In fact, if we agree that what is essential to modern letters consists of grasping the contingent as contingent, the primary motto of the age of science would be: no letter will ever abolish chance. And its secondary motto would be: every letter is a throw of the dice.

Letters are as they are, without there being any reason why they are as they are; at the same time, there is no reason why they should be otherwise than they are. And if they were otherwise than they are, they would just be other letters. In truth, from the moment that it exists, a letter remains the same and does not change ("the unique Number that cannot be another"). At most a discourse can—not change the letter, but choose other letters. Thus, letters deceptively appear to be immutable, like eternal ideas. No doubt, the immutability of what has no reason to be as it is has nothing to do with the immutability of that which cannot be otherwise than it is without violating reason. But the imaginary similarity remains.

From this it follows that, insofar as it can be otherwise, the ability of letters to grasp the realm of the diverse gives them the imaginary traits of what cannot be otherwise than it is. This is what we refer to as the necessity of the laws of science, which thoroughly resembles the Supreme Being's necessity, and all the more so by virtue of the fact that the former has nothing to do with the latter. The structure of modern science rests entirely on contingency. The material necessity granted to laws is the trace of this contingency itself. At first blush, each point of each referent for each of science's propositions appears to be able to be infinitely otherwise than it is, from an infinite number of points of view; ultimately, letters fix it into place as it is, as not being able to be otherwise than it is (except by changing letters, which is to say, only partially). But the condition for this last moment is, of course, the earlier moment. To demonstrate that a point in the universe is as it is requires that the dice of a possible universe are thrown in which this point would be other than it is.[31] The core doctrine (of science) has given a name to the time it takes for the dice to tumble before coming to a stop: the emergence of the subject, who is not the thrower (the thrower does not exist) but the dice themselves insofar as they are in suspension. In the vertigo of mutually exclusive possibilities the flash of the impossible finally appears, at the last moment, when the dice land. Once they have landed, it is impossible that their faces show a different number. Here we can see how the impossible is not disconnected from contingency, but makes up its real kernel.

To see this it would be necessary that one not stop moving from the first moment to the last, yet this is what cannot be done, because it would also be necessary to not cease going back to the first moment from the last. Science at any rate does not allow for this; once the letters are fixed, only necessity remains, which imposes the forgetting of the contingency that authorized them. The inopportuneness of the return of the contingent is what Lacan calls the "suture." The radicality of the forgetting is what Lacan calls "foreclosure" ("Science and Truth," Lacan 2006m, 742). Since the subject is what emerges in the move from the first moment to the last, suture and foreclosure are necessarily the suture and foreclosure of the subject.[32]

To admit that a contingent and empirical proposition is mathematizable, insofar as it is empirical and contingent, is to tear apart and stitch back together the unchangeable and the transitory in terms of letters; and it is to do so in an entirely unheard-of way, one that is incessantly precarious and incessantly reestablished. The entire set of points to which the propositions of science refer is usually called the universe. Since each of these points must be able to be grasped as a fluctuation of infinite variation, since all it takes for two possible universes to be distinct from each other is one variation in one of their points, since because of this fact there are an infinite number of possible universes, and since the universe only exists for science thanks to possible universes, the universe is necessarily infinite and could not possibly be otherwise, even if the points that make it up were to turn out to be actually finite in number. We could almost call this a qualitative infinity rather than a quantitative one.

Now, infinity is attributed to the universe only thanks to contingency, which comes to it from within. Once again, this disrupts the convention that puts infinity in an external location, transcendent to the universe. The universe, as the object of science and as a contingent object, is intrinsically infinite:[33]

The infinity of the universe is the mark of its radical contingency.

Hence, the attributes of infinity must be looked for within it, not beyond it. The modern thesis par excellence would thus be:

Finitude does not exist in the universe.

And since nothing exists except within the universe, it would also say:

Finitude does not exist.

Because:

There is nothing outside of the universe.

From which it follows, especially, that the subject is not something beyond the universe. How, despite this, the subject can and must still be distinct from the universe is what the theory of the subject is about. We can see why it needs to use the mathematical theory of the internal and the external: in other words, topology. We can also see why it contains all the variants of internal exclusion ("Science and Truth," Lacan 2006m, 731). These are necessary consequences of science's Core Doctrine. We can also see why science's Core Doctrine has to be connected to hypotheses on the subject, independently of any historical correlation. The hypothesis of the subject of science can be detached from historicism.

It is difficult to imagine that there is nothing outside of the universe. This is why figures of what is beyond the universe continually recur among our representations: God, Man, the Ego, to which some special property is attributed that exempts them from the universe and makes the universe into a Whole. This special property goes by different names: for a long time philosophy went with the soul, which links humanity to God. But the soul is part of the ancient world and *epistèmè*. When these gave way to modern science, the soul also gradually had to be given up. Then came consciousness.

This is where psychoanalysis has an impact. Psychoanalysis takes up the problem of the universe and resolves it in the following manner. The concept that there is a universe, from which nothing is excepted, not even Man, is a concept that rejects consciousness: it is the unconscious. In this respect, the word "unconscious," with its negative prefix, makes sense. If consciousness and, more precisely, self-consciousness gather together all the privileges of humanity, as an exception from the Whole, the negation with which Freud affects consciousness has only one purpose: to render these privileges obsolete. This also affects the soul, and this sheds light on why Lacan, taking a step further than Freud, tries to cross it out: see *Television* (Lacan 1990a [1973], 6). He is just following through with something implicit in the word "unconscious." At the same time that the soul is attacked, the figure of God, who is beyond-the-universe par excellence, is too. This explains Lacan's *logion* "God is unconscious": it means first and foremost this: the word "unconscious" stands for the inexistence of anything that might be considered beyond-the-universe; but the name "God" designates something beyond-the-universe; the triumph of the modern universe over the worlds of antiquity is thus that the unconscious even wins out over God.

But this *logion* itself is entirely connected to modern science and to the apparatus of the universe. The fact that science requires the universe, and that the universe renders any beyond-the-universe impossible . . . the single word "unconscious" stands for all of this, and in one blow both the soul and God are a-theitized. Conversely, a system of propositions that would aim at an object defined as unconscious can only be brought about in modern science and in the universe that it founds. Rabelais gave us the expression "science without conscience," and for this reason alone it was the ruin of the soul. Or, even more accurately, science is only completed when it makes itself into the science of the fact that there is no consciousness and no soul.[34]

It is strictly the case, as Freud affirmed, that psychoanalysis wounds the Ego and that this is what links it to Copernicus, that is, to modern science. But in order to understand this, we must add that narcissism can always be taken as a demand for an exception for oneself—and conversely. The hypothesis of the unconscious is just another way to affirm that such exceptions do not exist; for this very reason, it is nothing more and nothing less than an affirmation of the universe of science. Not only does the unconscious thus bring about the program that Rabelais feared, but it turns out to take on very precisely the functions of the infinite.

Furthermore, the two words have the same structure: one says *unbewusst* in the same way that one says *unendlich*. The infinite is the rejection of any exception to finitude; the unconscious is the rejection of the privilege of consciousness. Of course, Lacan often commented unfavorably on the negative character of the word *unbewusst*. This is a Cartesian view: the infinite is first and positive, while the finite is second and is obtained in some sense by subtraction; likewise, the unconscious explains consciousness, not the other way around. It stands for an affirmation and not a limitation. However, we can see that negation has its virtues.

The German language even enhances them. In German the prefix *un-* is not always as flatly negative as the Latin prefix *in-*; it is not limited to designating the complementary class of the domain signified by the positive term. Thus, the *Unmensch* is not a non-human, but a botched human, a monster; the *Unkraut* is a plant (*Kraut*), but a bad plant, a weed; the *unheimlich* is not the inverse of the familiar, but something familiar infected with an anxiety that shatters it.[35] Likewise, one could easily say that in the modern universe the finite and the infinite are not domains that need to be distinguished from each other. Instead, the infinite incessantly infects the finite, in the sense that everything finite, insofar as science deals with it, is first posited as being able to be infinitely other than it is. Moreover, this would not take us very far from Descartes, the theoretician of eternal truths. Similarly, in psychoanalysis, the unconscious incessantly undermines consciousness; it shows how it is able to be otherwise than it is, and it is only in this way that it establishes how precisely it cannot be otherwise. The negative prefix is just the sign of this infection.

Psychoanalysis is fundamentally a doctrine of the infinite and contingent universe. This explains its views on death and sexuality.

We cannot ignore the fact that for most people death is the very mark of finitude. But the modern lemma holds that finitude does not exist, and psychoanalysis adheres to this lemma. It even gives a specific version of it:

> *Insofar as it is a mark of finitude, death is nothing in analysis;*

or:

> *Death only counts in analysis insofar as it is a mark of the infinite;*

or:

> *Death is nothing except the object of a drive.*

The concept of the death drive is based on this, and we can conclude that the word *death* is a focal point of the homonymy between the finite and infinite. In addition, we can conclude that any philosophy in which death counts as the inverse—as the mark of finitude—is incompatible with the possibility of psychoanalysis. A specific conclusion: if Heidegger's philosophy is one of these, if being towards death is being towards finitude, then, despite the exchanges of letters and private visits, despite even the importance that the definition of truth as unveiling has for the doctrine of the cure, Lacan's doctrine, as a doctrine of psychoanalysis, is contradictory to Heidegger's philosophy—and vice versa.

Psychoanalysis deals with what the moderns call sexuality. Everybody knows this. However, we can wonder why, and in what respect, it deals with it. It is useless to say that sexuality exists empirically, so there must be some discourse that speaks reasonably about it. Because it is precisely not trivial that sexuality exists—that is, that a determinable region of reality bears this name. This is so little the case that it has become, it seems, unacceptable nowadays to even raise the question. Foucault learned how much it cost him to be a revisionist on this point. Even supposing that sexuality exists as it is said to, it is not clear that psychoanalysis speaks about it directly. We know that educated minds—Jung was anything but ignorant—have denied it.

I will put forward the idea that sexuality, insofar as psychoanalysis speaks about it, is nothing other than this: the mark of infinite contingency on the body. That there is sexuation rather than not is contingent. That there are two sexes rather than one or several is contingent. That someone falls on one side or the other is contingent. That sexuation is linked to certain bodily traits is contingent. That certain cultural characteristics are linked to these is contingent. Because it is contingent, it touches on the infinite.

However, there is something that does not cease to be able to be put into letters, since the names "man" and "woman" are first of all a way to include oneself within a set that is both totalizable and open, and since there is a certain type of logic to this inclusion. In 1945, "Logical Time and the Assertion of Anticipated Certainty" (Lacan 2006c) calls it a collective logic and proposes a dialectical version of it, one that could be dramatized in a quasi-Sartrean way (it is not far from *No Exit*); it is found again in "L'Étourdit" (Lacan 2001f [1972], 458–66), stripped of drama and formalized in a quasi-Russellian way. This explains why the question of the limit is pivotal for the latter, as well as why it is connected to the question of the infinite. The formulas of sexuation are about an infinite Whole, affected by the existence or inexistence of a limit.

The Freudian unconscious, as sexual, is the unconscious insofar as it could be otherwise than it is; it is also the unconscious insofar as it is as it is and about which, from the moment that it is as it is, letters state that it from then on cannot be otherwise than it is. But the unconscious is infinite at the same time. In it, then, the infinite and the contingent meet, as they should. But sexuality is also infected by infinity; this is the case because of the death drive, because of *jouissance*, and again because of contingency, of the troubles of the Whole. This is the case to such an extent that there is a complete reversibility: the unconscious is the infinite universe's grip on the speaking being's thought, but as such it can only be sexual; sexuality is the infinite universe's grip on the speaking being's body, but as such it can only be unconscious. This gets us back to modern science. Psychoanalysis can only authorize itself on the basis of science's Core Doctrine on the condition that it bases itself on sexuation as a phenomenon and on sexuality as the region of reality in which this phenomenon can be grasped. Science's Core Doctrine, conversely, is just another name for sexuation as a throw of the dice, that is to say, as letter.

3

The First Lacanian Classicism

1. Language and the Break

The entirety of science's Core Doctrine, its theorems, its hypotheses, and its lemmas, is highly significant. It allows us to sketch out the space of Lacanian doctrinal statements more precisely than we otherwise could. If considered carefully, it could offer us a way to analyze what has sometimes been called the thought of the 1960s. Because this thought, among its many other characteristics, in particular agreed on one axiomatic thesis: "there are breaks."[1] It understood this in a historicizing sense. Of course, later on the Core Doctrine will understand it differently. But it is also true that in the 1960s it agreed with the common interpretation.

The existential axiom that there are breaks, and its chronological reading, are not anything new in themselves. Since the lightning-like aphorisms of Saint Paul, announcing the end of the ancient world he himself was bringing to a close ("As for the Greeks, they search for wisdom," 1 Cor. 1:22), they can be found, in different forms, in a number of authors. Men and women of letters in the French language incessantly commented on the antecedents and the aftermath of the French Revolution in these terms, such that the axiom that there are breaks became for them a political litmus test. For some, to affirm it was almost as important as activism itself. The 1960s just give us a particular version of this.

In *Writing Degree Zero* Barthes essentially states the thesis that "literature is intrinsically modern." Thus it has a before, and perhaps an after. This modernity begins, roughly, with the advent of the bourgeoisie as an economically and politically dominant class. At least in France. We could easily conclude from this that French literature provides us with the very model for Literature, just as the English Industrial Revolution, according to some, provides us with the very model for capitalist industry. According to Barthes's own logic, the break called Literature can and must be linked to others: he mentions the social and political break of the sixteenth century, and the one at the end of the eighteenth century. Nothing rules out the possibility that Koyré's break is also pertinent to it. Barthes just did not connect the two.

Althusser did, or at least he established the terms in which it could be done. His project rests on the following hypothesis:

The universe of modern science is coextensive with the world market.

From this it follows that shedding light on the material foundations of the latter also clarifies the basis of the former's legitimacy—and vice versa. But the notion of the universe and the notion of science go together; neither goes without the other; only science can be the theory of the universe; the object of science can be nothing other than the universe. At the same time, a complete theory of the world market would be a theory of capitalism. In this way, the theory of capitalism and the doctrine of modern science are partially connected. Contrary to what Althusser himself often held, this is the case not just because Marx, by writing *Capital*, was part of the movement of science—this is undeniable, but insufficient. The relationship is more fundamental, and it affects the conditions of possibility for Marx's oeuvre itself—more exactly, the foundations of his research program and the definition of its object.[2]

So, thanks to Marx, and in a way that owes nothing to the Sartrean progressivism of the 1950s, a constellation of mutually connected theses is established. They help us to see what was specific to the 1960s. It does not consist in the affirmation that there are breaks, but rather in the discursive function that is given to this affirmation. Breaks are, explicitly or not, taken to be analogous in the universe of thought to the historical caesuras theorized by Marxism. They allow a formal relationship to Marxism to be preserved without having to remain subjected to it in substance.

This is not the place to go into the discursive mechanics thanks to which the political progressivism that Sartre represented so well gradually gave way to propositions that increasingly separated political choices from intellectual choices.[3] It suffices to establish in what way science's Core Doctrine, even though it is not fundamentally historicizing, contains logics both consistent and complete that are found elsewhere in an explicitly historicizing form.

In order to get to this point we should consider Foucault first. In the conjuncture we are considering he alone, in fact, developed a significant variation. We can say that, better than anyone else, he understood the affiliations that I am pointing out. Whether he also accepted science's Core Doctrine, or more simply the system of links that the Core Doctrine is able to generate . . . this deserves some examination.

In fact, it is not even certain that he accepted the existential axiom of breaks. Or rather, he accepted it, but only in order to fragment it immediately into a group of problems: what is a break, how is one recognized, are there different types, etc. Foucault's program thus constructed a general typology of any possible discursive break: a sort of topology of the concept, if topology is indeed the science of borders, exteriors, interiors, and overlaps.

Foucault, ultimately, did not grant himself History. Even if he maintained chronological seriation as a last-instance determination, even if he admitted such a thing as discursive succession, even if it must always be homologous to a temporal succession, even if the compatibility of discourses must let itself be interpreted as a (chronological) proximity (a period), even then it is the case that the pivot points are weakened; the names antiquity, Middle Ages, and modern times appear now and then, but they are struck with a principled suspicion that does not prohibit their use, but requires that they be submitted to critical, preferably unexpected, inspection. It is true that by keeping to chronology, Foucault does keep the word "history," but it is banalized and subjugated to the genitives that follow it: history of madness, history of bodies, history of sexuality. These syntagms include and reveal an insolence addressed to absolute usages of history, whether singular ("to think History," "to make History") or plural ("*Bibliothèque des histoires*").[4]

Foucault preferred to give the name *archaeology* to his method, which was at once clarifying and risky. Clarifying because this word is precisely not that of history, which would say more than is permissible; risky because it closely connects the general theory of the break to a theory of layers and overlaps. The claim that a discontinuity is necessarily covered over by a layer that hides it is a nontrivial hypothesis. It cannot be said that it has been demonstrated; it is, however, consubstantial with the very word "archaeology."

In any case, Foucault's general theory is not sufficient for science's Core Doctrine: it is thus not sufficient to authorize Lacan's discourse. It is not sufficient in the strict sense: it does not contain all the axioms that Lacan needs. This means that, with respect to Foucault, Lacan contains extra axioms. History is not one of them: Foucault does not grant it to himself, but Lacan refuses it. No incompatibility there. The point of dissent is elsewhere, and it concerns breaks as such.

In fact, Foucault's theory tends to be radically skeptical about breaks—not, again, about their existence (even supposing that they are not axiomatic, they are proven by the successes of the investigations that assume them), but about their possible types: Kojève and Koyré's theses, which are deemed to be useless and risky, are consciously and readily rejected: all that is assumed, axiomatic or not, is the existential affirmation "there are breaks." The rest is an empirical matter.

But this affirmation, according to Foucault, only posits (1) that there are heterogeneities among discourses, and (2) that these heterogeneities leave locatable and datable traces in the archive (a chronology, rather than a history). It does not assume that these traces can be gathered together into general simultaneities. It remains entirely possible that the heterogeneous cuts affecting discourse A do not at the same time affect discourse B, which, however, is compossible with A.

But combining Koyré and Kojève's propositions does seem to affirm that there is a certain break that affects not only two discourses— like science and metaphysics—but *all* compossible discourses. This is what the use of totalizing terms like *world* and *universe* obviously implies ("the world of approximation," "the universe of the exact").[5] Let's call a break like this *major*. Science's Core Doctrine can then be reformulated in this way:

> *The break between* epistème *and modern science is a major break.*

This at least is the reading that Lacan gives it; it is required if the Core Doctrine has to include a theory of the modern subject (the hypothesis of the subject of science); it is even more strongly required if, as it seems that Lacan wished, it has to be joined, as a lemma, to Althusser's hypothesis. (Lacan was not directly interested in Barthes, although he himself advanced propositions on style that are, thanks to Norden, largely compatible with *Writing Degree Zero*.)

This can be put differently: according to Lacan, the word "modern" does not stand for anything if it does not stand for a major break.

The elements of this break are certainly open to debate, but there is no doubt that if it is assumed, it is assumed to affect all compossible discourses: not one of them is immune to it, at least insofar as they are all modern. Neither the material economy (Althusser's hypothesis) nor letters (Barthes's hypothesis and Lacan's equivalent hypothesis), neither political philosophies (L. Strauss or C. Schmitt), nor images (Panofsky), nor speculative philosophy (Heidegger). Finally, not consciousness: the emergence of psychoanalysis testifies to the fact that inner life itself is not immune to the break; the subject is not an empire within an empire; there is a modern subject (whether one distinguishes it from ancient subjectivity, or whether one assumes that subjectivity is born with modernity itself); psychoanalysis is both the proof and the effect of its establishment.

In other words, and it is time to emphasize this, the configuration of science's Core Doctrine is based on a supplementary existential axiom:

> *Not only are there breaks, there are major breaks.*

But Foucault, of course, does not grant this at all. He even seems to assume the contrary. His entire project is based on the possible noncoincidence and non-homology of breaks; whence the constant decouplings, setbacks, and turbulences that must never be overlooked.

So Christianity may be a break in the history of sexuality, but not necessarily one in that of madness. The Galileism of the beginning of the seventeenth century may be a break in the science of nature, but not in the discourses that touch on speaking, classification, and exchange. The latter are marked by another break, which dates from the end of the eighteenth century and which seems indifferent to mathematized physics. As equally radical as they are, each of these breaks takes the properties of a major break away from the others. Even breaks that are contemporary (or nearly so)—for example, Galileism and the Great Confinement—are not necessarily connected to each other. This is even the constitutive illusion of the "psy-" discourses (of which psychoanalysis is a part, according to Foucault): to believe in a connection between the theory of private processes and the theory of public processes.

Generally speaking, it is always possible for a discourse to be immune to the breaks that the vulgate considers to be major: Christianity, capitalism, and modern science. It is always possible that breaks are out of sync with each other, even when they are, according to historians, simultaneous. Moreover, we would not have to push Foucault's consistency too far to find a political suspicion motivating his view: the figure of the major break contains all the traits of what political discourse has called "Revolution." We can even add: just as modern science is supposed to be born from a scientific revolution, modern political discourse is notable for having constructed the model of the Revolution, and for using it as a standard for any possible political goal. But, according to Foucault, Revolution does not exist: to believe in it leads to catastrophe, in practice and in theory. Similarly, the discursive figure of the major break, no matter how less guilty it is (apparently we cannot attribute any massacres to it), is nonetheless misleading.

Thus a break is radically multiple; or rather, it is the multiple itself. Often going unnamed—Foucault did not like to speak of breaks—it is etched into the heart of nominations, whose system it articulates. Foucault was the first to have placed discourse within the regime of names alone; the first to have consistently tried to sketch them out on the basis of their compatibilities and incompatibilities alone. However, he did not give in to the temptation that always haunts such a move: to hold that ultimately there is just one discourse, because any name is as good as any other. He never gave up on the multiplicity of discourses: that is, on the heterogeneity of names, on their inequality. Breaks designate nothing else.

Breaks are just the rejection of overabundant synonymy, and they multiply in number to the jerky rhythm of what they reject. This explains René Char's aphorism, which Foucault put on the back cover of *The History of Sexuality*: "The history of men is the long succession of synonyms for the same vocable. To contradict it is a duty."[6] In other words, breaks are discursive rebellions; their sudden appearances are as sprawled out as uprisings themselves are; they have more to do with 1968 than with 1917; the existential axiom gives way to a commandment that is both ethical and political: "it is always right to rebel against synonyms."[7]

If there are not any major breaks, then there are systems of breaks that are independent of each other and not synchronous. For every discourse affected by a break, there would always be at least another one that, at that same time, is not. By means of an intelligent, if not cunning, methodology, every discourse can thus one by one be used as a sound reference point. There is no need to assume an absolute reference point that would be essentially beyond any break, since disharmonies and turbulences are sufficient in order for locations to be mutually figured out.

Unless, by chance (but it is the circumstances that decide this), a certain amount of passion turns some empirical configuration into an absolute reference point for just a moment. This explains the interventions Foucault often made in newspapers. They depend entirely on his core doctrinal axiomatic ("there are no major breaks") but are corrected by a practical maxim in the Kantian sense: "there are some circumstances that, in the heat of the moment, have the effects of major breaks and absolute reference points."

Foucault gave a name to these effects that resemble truth-effects, although they aren't. In his work on prisons he developed the concept of "intolerance-inquiries": by means of the most rigorous research, shed light on an empirical object (the activities of an apparatus, the proposals of one of its agents, open or hidden decisions, etc.) so that it awakens for those who become aware of it an intolerance-point: the judgment, prior to any declaration, that such a thing can no longer be tolerated. The intellectual is taken to have no other ethical maxim but to proffer statements that are able to bring about such a judgment in those who proffer nothing.

We can now understand this move and this language: the point is to return to this intolerance-point, found within the limits of the inquiry, as if one were returning to it from an external point situated beyond a major break (unless there are neither external points nor major breaks), based solely on the totality of discourses (unless this totality cannot be constructed), and evaluate it (unless this evaluation is authorized only by its pure and simple enunciation—itself ephemeral).

However, if Lacan was right—if there really are major breaks—then mutual references are impossible; we need a sound reference point that is immune to breaks. This reference point must at least allow us to deal with homonymies and the suspensions of synonyms, to which, in their simplest form, the breaks boil down. The question of this immunity's location is not explicitly dealt with by Koyré, Kojève, or Lacan.

In the historicizing reading there is however a first, apparently simple, answer; there is at least one set of realities that are immune to breaks, and these are languages. Relative to discourses and their displacements and discontinuities, a given language is the place where homonymies can be grasped. In fact, only a language can be such a place.

In other words, the assumption that there are major breaks is also the assumption that they do not affect language. But this is nothing other than what Stalin sought to establish. We can even say that according to his own version of Marxist scholasticism he succeeded, to the point that it is correct to speak of a veritable Stalin-theorem.[8] In Marxist doctrine, it states (along with its converse): "there are changes of infrastructure that do not lead to changes in language; there are changes in language that do not depend on changes in infrastructure"; but, given this doctrine, any change in infrastructure affects, directly or indirectly, in a more or less perceptible manner, every super-structural agency, without exception; this amounts to saying that every infrastructural change is a major break. Classical Marxism assumes that only a change in infrastructure can produce a major break. Stalin's theorem can thus be reformulated as follows: "language is immune to major breaks" (or, in political language: "language is immune to revolutions").[9]

Obviously, this theorem is true only of language as *form*; it is easily refuted when it comes to what is not formal about language, and Stalin knew this better than anyone. He assumes then that language as form exists, and that it can be opposed to language as substance. But language as form is what linguistics, in Stalin's day, called "structure." Jakobson even agreed with this theorem and supported it.

In referring to structure ("the unconscious is structured like a language"), Lacan stakes out a position on the question of the absolute reference point, and he appears to do so in the same way as Stalin. Of course, this does not exhaust the significance of his relationship to structuralism. But the fact remains that his relationship to structuralism also entails this relationship to Stalin.

Whence the relationship that Lacan thought he could work out: if what Lacan says of language is true, then Marxism may be true, even if it is not so necessarily; if what Marxism—that is to say Stalin—says of language is true, then Lacan is necessarily true.[10]

But in fact, the relationship is even more intimate than this: it is not only a matter of language, but indeed of science's Core Doctrine; in the historicizing reading of it, the Core Doctrine requires Stalin's theorem (as well as what we can call Stalin's lemma: "language, as form, is the reference point that allows major breaks to be discerned"). This is required to the exact extent that it depends on Kojève's theorem. This shows that, despite what he no doubt thought, Kojève depends on Stalin *the theoretician* and not just Stalin as the mythical figure of the Emperor of the modern world.[11]

There's more. Going beyond the texts themselves, and no doubt beyond the full awareness of the authors, we can find in Stalin's theorem something that can help us resolve a difficulty in science's Core Doctrine. Many authors have noticed how the status of mathematics and logic are problematic in it. There is an open question here: Is mathematics itself affected by the Galilean break? The most generally agreed-upon answer is no. There is not, according to most authorities (Bourbaki, for example) an absolute break between Greek mathematics and Cartesian or Cantorian mathematics; there are differences, certainly, but nothing that compares to the relationship between pre-Galilean and post-Galilean physics. This amounts to affirming that mathematics is in exactly the right position to function as a reference point for the major break.

Mathematics is not a Galilean science; it is not a Popperian science; it is not concerned with the contingent. This is explained precisely by the role that it plays in the break. The immunity of mathematics to the major break is at the very heart of the break itself.

We see, then, that mathematics strictly speaking has the same status as language does, according to Stalin's theorem. And we know, moreover, that defining mathematics in terms of language has become prevalent among moderns. True, it is already present in Galileo: to make mathematics into the alphabet (and of course not the hieroglyph) of the universe is to confer upon it *in nuce* a status that will turn out, at the end of a long, winding development, to be rather generally accepted. That mathematics is a language (moreover, most moderns hold that it falls to logic to state its rules, on the condition that logic itself is put in a mathematical language) is an affirmation that connects gracefully to science's

Core Doctrine, and resolves the paradox according to which a break can be recognized by what escapes it. This is not the place to determine whether this is a tenable position. The important point for now is to see in it a misrecognized version of Stalin's theorem.

In light of this, to interpret science's Core Doctrine in historicizing terms, to attribute to mathematics a continuity that is immune to major breaks, to recognize in mathematics something that is constitutive of the major break of the modern universe, to define mathematics in terms of language, to be a Stalinist on matters of language . . . these turn out to be five interconnected positions.

Foucault's theory is entirely different; it can perfectly well accommodate the hypothesis that languages do not escape from the disjointed and turbulent breaks that are theorized by archaeology. An anti-Stalinist in political matters, Foucault was also anti-Stalinist regarding language. More exactly, he refrained from pronouncing any judgment on languages: for him, it is impossible to determine if they are superstructures or not. It is true that good little Foucauldians have shown less reserve; but this hardly matters.

This explains why Foucault never engaged, except prudently, in lines of reasoning that were common among his colleagues: drawing a conclusion about the appearance or disappearance of things based on the appearance or disappearance of words. That a word begins to exist or ceases to exist is a fact that he makes use of, but with striking discretion. In truth, we could say that some of Foucault's major works depend on the inverse hypothesis: the same word "madness" and the same word "prison" appear on both sides of the break that affects the discourses in which they appear. It is true that other statements, more local, depend on exactly the inverse hypothesis; thus the emergence of the noun phrase *mental illness* is a signal that Foucault's method deems relevant.

This is because languages [*la langue*] are not important to Foucault, nor is language [*le langage*], whether considered as form or as substance. It is true that linguistics provided him with concepts and supports, but it is doubtful that these were anything more than analogies authorized by the conjuncture of the 1960s. It is equally true that words and phrases are the material causes of discourses. But discourses follow their own law, which owes nothing to whatever laws govern words and phrases. The law of discourses comes down to one alone: "there are discontinuities" or "synonyms must be rejected." This, then, is the only object that can be dealt with, by a sort of vortex physics in which nothing exists that could be considered absolute. Just as Descartes only allowed for relative motions.

By way of contrast, we can better determine the nature of Lacanian doctrine. Not only are there discontinuities, but there are discontinuities that affect all discourses. This assumes that there are such things as absolute movements and, at the same time, that there is something like an absolute reference point.

We evoked Stalin for good reason. His is the name that should be found hidden underneath that of the linguist Jakobson: the affirmation that the absolute reference point is the structure of natural languages, independently of both base and superstructure. By this very fact it is able to be grouped together into one single formal concept: language. But with Stalin, even if he is covered over by Jakobson, one sticks with History. Lacan, however, does not believe in History, even though he allows for major breaks.

The connections are inexorable here. If the major break is interpreted in historicizing terms, then Stalin is necessary; he can only be avoided if a non-historicizing interpretation is developed.

This is indeed why Lacan felt it important to not only focus on language. He evokes it explicitly only to leave it behind at the very moment that he focuses on it. The absolute reference point is not language in itself nor the languages into which it is polymerized, but that of which language, reduced to its real, is the place-holder. That is to say, the subject.

We again find here the theory of four discourses, and their importance can now be better evaluated. Not only does it propose a non-chronological theory of discontinuities, not only does it propose a theory of the absolute properties of any discourse whatsoever, not only does it allow for absolute movement ("the quarter turn"), but it determines and names the absolute reference point on which it rests.

Science's Core Doctrine assumes this absolute reference point due to the very fact that it requires that there be major breaks. On the other hand, it is also combined with a theory of discourses according to which no break is chronological. The Core Doctrine thus affirms that major breaks are not chronological. In relation to them, the absolute reference point does not have the distinctive property of avoiding chronology. Since the non-chronological theory of breaks depends on a theory of places, the reference point's key attribute must be found in its a-topia: its ability to occupy any place whatsoever, wherever it happens to insist. The only real that presents, by definition and by construction, these key attributes—a-topia and insistence—is the subject of the signifier. This is why Koyré and Kojève's theorems are only fully grounded if the hypothesis of the subject of science and the definition of the subject as the subject of a signifier are also admitted. Modern science, insofar as it is science and insofar as it is modern, does thus determine a mode of the subject's constitution.

Again, this hypothesis itself needs to be radically de-historicized. This is what the theory of psychoanalytic discourse allows us to do. To claim that there are major breaks is to claim that, when it comes to the subject, all synonyms are completely suspended. The doctrine of interpretation—of the cure—finds herein the basis of its own legitimacy; it could not have any others. An interpretation is just that: put forth the word that will make it the case that between the before and the after, nothing is synonymous. A word can only accomplish this if it touches the subject. There is thus no interpretation except at the point of the subject. But this subject-point is the very thing that a general doctrine of breaks requires, insofar as a break suspends synonyms. Science's Core Doctrine is in part connected to what appears to be the most intimate kernel of Freudian practice, whose matrix is exposed by the theory of discourses under the heading of psychoanalytic discourse. We may then go back to the equation of subjects, and we can finally understand its reach: "the *praxis* of psychoanalysis is interpretation; the subject that psychoanalysis requires—insofar as it interprets—is the subject that science requires insofar as it is constituted by a major break: every major break has the structure of an interpretation."[12]

This is the only way to surpass the power of Stalin—that is to say, of Marx.

2. The Paradigm of Structure

It turns out that, in Lacan's configuration, what Stalin and Jakobson promoted under the heading of languages or the linguistic is in fact just the strict place-holder for the subject, which neither Stalin nor Jakobson were in a position to speak about adequately. The doctrine of the unconscious, insofar as it is structured like a language, allows us to go from languages to the subject. To understand this is to understand the relationship to structuralism.

Lacan is a structuralist figure. This is not in any doubt, if we follow conventional wisdom. What this means still needs to be clarified. It means that we have to explain more clearly than is ordinarily the case how Lacan relates to the structuralist program, which in turn means that we have to explain, more clearly than is ordinarily the case, what this program is.

Lacan himself deemed it useful to reassert his own doctrine just before it was more widely disseminated: "this correction," he said in 1965, "affects the status of everything that is grouped together, too widely now, under the heading of structuralism" (Lacan 2001b [1965], 188). A reciprocal gesture has hardly ever been made.[13] Now is a good time for one.

Structuralism, apart from being a fashionable enthusiasm, was a shape that science took on: a moment when it was thought that the jurisdiction of modern science could and should be extended far beyond the limits that had long been given to it.

Consider the ideal of science, the mathematized science of the universe. Consider also, as a representative of that ideal science, the form issuing from the nineteenth century and the beginnings of the twentieth, according to which there could be only one standard for mathematization: exact quantitative *measure*. On this basis, an empirical discourse is thought to be mathematized if and only if its propositions consist of measurements or numerical reference points. Since Galileo's time, the sciences that take as their object parts of the realm of nature have adhered to this definition; when it comes to social or more generally human objects, adaptations have been necessary. These have taken on different forms: preserving the ideal of measurement (by using statistical procedures, for example), abandoning it and replacing it with another ideal figure, or renouncing any ideal at all.

Structuralism emerges from this conflict; it adheres to the ideal of science, but it proposes a new form for it; it makes two changes to the ideal science; one involves empirical objects: structuralism deals with human objects—this is why the opposition between nature and culture is essential for it.

The second involves mathematization, which must henceforth be understood in a new way: it is no longer a matter of measurement, *stricto sensu*, but of a rendering into letters [*littéralisation*] and a nonquantitative dissolution of the qualitative. This is a reinterpretation of Koyré's third theorem (chapter 2, p. 21).

Recall that modern science, compared to Aristotelian physics, takes on a difficult task; that of eliminating qualities from science. Not only practical qualities like the good, the bad, the useful, the pleasant, etc.—but also and especially sensible qualities: fast, heavy, colored, warm, etc. Such is the first move it makes: this is not enough to count as a mathematizing, but it is a necessary step. Only thanks to it could mathematically literalized propositions take pride of place. When all is said and done, qualities would no longer need to appear, except as secondary stand-ins coming from ordinary language.

Physics says nothing directly about the warm and cold; it says something about the movements of molecules, some of which can be associated with the sensible property that is commonly called warm. Likewise, it says nothing about lightness and darkness, but it says something about light and the configurations that can be associated with the sensible properties commonly called lightness and darkness. It says nothing of colors, but it says something about what supports them for beings who are endowed with vision.

In its own way, structuralism in linguistics is also a method that reduces sensible qualities. This can only be done in a limited way, since natural languages only involve sensible matter in one respect: the phonic form. Now, in this domain the method has obvious results.

Let's consider an example that has become famous: Trubetzkoy's suggestion for how to deal with stop consonants in German. A word like *Rad* ("wheel") turns out to be a homonym with *Rat* ("counsel"); in the two cases, phonetics registers a [t], [rat]. When we spell them, however, we put a *d* in the first and a *t* in the second; the plural, moreover, confirms that this is correct: in *Räder* ("wheels") the /d/ becomes audible and in *Räte* ("counsels") the /t/ does. If, as it seems that we must admit, *Rad* in the singular and *Räder* in the plural are one and the same word, something must be said about what happens to the /d/. Some linguists will then say that "the /d/ in German is voiceless at the end of a word."

According to a strict method, Trubetzkoy objects, this claim is inexact and imprecise: the stop consonants of *Rad* and *Rat* are indeed materially voiceless, but this is not the case from a scientific point of view. In fact, they cannot be opposed to a materially voiced stop since these do not even appear in this position. Linguistic properties only exist to the strict extent to which they make up part of a distinctive oppositional relationship. The final element of *Rad* and *Rat* is, in the strict sense, neuter and without any voiced property. Generally speaking, a phonic entity cannot, from the point of view of science, be voiceless (or voiced, or labial, or dental, etc.) in and of itself; it is so only by virtue of the difference that separates it from some other entity.

In the *Rad/Rat* example, the stop is said to be an entity called an *archiphoneme*, which possesses no value from the point of view of the oppositional property voiceless/voiced, and it is written, in capital letters, /T/. Both words will thus be written: /raT/.[14]

To hold this is to say that the sensible given counts for nothing, or it counts as something that is merely able to be recorded by phonetic apparatuses. Because it remains the case that the final phonic element of *Rat* and of *Rad* is "objectively" voiceless, that is, voiceless for the ear. But the practitioners of structural phonology point out that they were trained not to take this quality into account.

We find here a move characteristic of mathematized physics, even when it is not strictly Galilean.[15] Of course, quality is not being reduced to quantity; nor is it dissipated entirely; of course, it is not being reduced to geometric figures, but it is integrated into a tableau in which distances, proportions, and symmetries can be determined; of course it is not expressed in a numerical calculus, but it is nonetheless being rendered into letters [*une littéralisation*]: the very fact of writing the archiphoneme with a capital /T/ is a decision that is part of a system of notation as rigorous as algebraic notation's is, although it is incomparably less sophisticated.

It is correct to see this as an extended mathematization; it certainly wishes to be rigorous and constraining, but also relatively autonomous with respect to the mathematical apparatus *stricto sensu*—geometry, arithmetic, set theory (naive or abstract), mathematical structure, etc. We know that the linguistics of the 1920s was working toward this goal. At the end of it all, in the 1950s, it could be considered a discipline as literal as algebra or logic and yet entirely independent of them. On these foundations, it enjoyed empirical successes. With its method, the set of natural languages was thought to be graspable in its extension and in its detail. It could thus be thought that linguistics behaved just like a Galilean science did with its object. An extended Galileism, then, founded on an extended mathematics, and extended to unexpected objects.

For this object was language: that is to say, that which is primary in separating the human species from the realm of nature, such as it is generally understood, at least.[16] Lévi-Straussian anthropology also seemed to show that when applied to eminently nonnatural objects—kinship systems— similar methods led to an exhaustive, exact, precise, and demonstrative presentation of functions. The support that Lévi-Strauss found in linguistics is based on an analogy among procedures, and especially on an analogy among constitutive points of view.

We know that on this double foundation, in linguistics and anthropology, a whole movement in thought was launched; contrary to what has often been maintained, there is no doubt about its methodological unity, and its epistemological importance is not in doubt either. It is eminently reasonable that Lacan, whose relation to Galileism was a matter of principle and who moreover took his object to be more on the side of culture than nature (this was not necessarily the case for Freud), is included among the ranks of the structuralists.

The Rome Discourse has to be read in this light. It can be considered a genuine manifesto. An attentive reader will not fail to hear in it the accents of Rabelais's famous letter: "For that time was darksome, obscured with clouds of ignorance, and savouring a little of the infelicity and calamity of the Goths, who had, wherever they set foot, destroyed all good literature, which in my age hath by the divine goodness been restored unto its former light and dignity. . . . Now is it that the minds of men are qualified with all manner of discipline, and the old sciences revived which for many ages were extinct: now it is that the learned languages are to their pristine purity restored" (*Pantagruel*, chap. VIII, 249–50). It is true that Rabelais goes back to ancient science; for good reason he could not be Galilean, but he was Erasmian, as the break itself is in certain respects. That is to say, he upholds the ideal of literal precision, at a time when the study of nature was still characterized by approximation. From Erasmus to Galileo, we know that the transition is sound.

To such an extent that, thanks to the virtues of linguistic structuralism, one could believe that after many centuries of separation they were finally joined together. Never before had the ideal of precision in languages and the ideal of precision in Nature been brought this close together, and simultaneously proclaimed. The hour of a second Pantagruel had thus indeed arrived, to whom the birth of a new type of Galileism is announced, one more extensive than the former since it includes culture, and is founded, like it, on the "mathematical characters" Galileo spoke of. But these letters are not those of *measurement*, they are that of a *calculus*. It is true that in the meantime mathematics itself, taken in the strictest sense, is presented as a symbolism constrained by rules and disjoined from quantity.

Bourbaki provides us with the best proof of this. Lacan considers the kinship between his explicit literalization and the literalization of the linguists to be admissible. It is not necessary to conclude that mathematics is "applied" when it adapts itself to nonmeasurable objects, or that formulations other than mathematical ones are possible in linguistics or in anthropology. Instead, it is necessary to conclude that mathematics can expand its empire, without ceding anything about its essence. It is indeed a matter of an *extended Galileism*; one more extensive than the first, but also more rigorous, since it authorizes itself on the basis of a mathematics that is finally taken to the point of absolute literalism. Linguistics, deemed to be a completed science, only counts insofar as it proposes a mathematics.[17] Lacan the linguist is in fact Lacan the mathematician.

It is true that Lacan was really interested only in structural linguistics. However, this was not the only one among the possible forms of linguistics that presented itself in terms of mathematization. Others, even before

Chomsky, could have served as his reference point. After all, cutting-edge comparative grammar would have sufficed.

Moreover, it is obvious that after Chomsky linguistics counted less and less for Lacan; or, if it still counted, it no longer did in the same way. Lacan was a friend of Jakobson, he held Benveniste in esteem, but these relations were independent of the particular paradigm of which these two were a part. A more intrinsic kinship with structural linguistics must be identified. There must be specific theses that characterize structural linguistics as opposed to other linguistics—ones potentially more recent—that would be candidates able to represent a Galileism in language.

Structural linguistics is based on three minimalist theses:

1. A theory-minimalism: A theory draws closer and closer to the ideal of science the more it forces itself to use a minimal number of initial axioms and concepts in order to obtain a maximal descriptive power.
2. An object-minimalism: One will only come to know a language by forcing oneself to consider only the minimal properties that make it into a system, which can be broken down into elements that are themselves minimal.
3. A property-minimalism: The only properties that an element of a system has are those that are determined by the system.

Thesis 1 is in fact a return to the ancient axiomatic. It seems certain that theoreticians in linguistics—and especially the first among them, Saussure—did not have a clear awareness of this lineage; no doubt it appeared to be self-evident to them. But this is not the case at all. Quite to the contrary, it was rejected by the dogmatists of modern science: by Koyré implicitly, by Popper explicitly. Thus its reemergence is not without consequences.

Accordingly, the linguistics Lacan uses is paradoxical. Allegedly the harbinger of a new form of Galileism, it bases itself on a pre-Galilean form of science. The ideal science is not in sync with the ideal of science that it wishes to represent. This contributes to an instability that will affect extended Galileism. Nevertheless Lacan, in his very first move, does not seem to have been aware of it.

Thesis 2 obviously remains empty if nothing general is said about what a system is. The answer, as we know, goes back to Saussure: there is a system if and only if there is difference; given the minimalist thesis, nothing else needs to be considered when it comes to knowing a language except difference. It turns out that *structure* is the term for a system that is reduced to its minimal relations; the word *structuralism* designates a theory based on this.

That being said, it must be obvious that the property of being a system thus defined in minimal terms is not something specific to languages. Structuralism can in principle be extended to other objects; in fact, to the totality of cultural objects. The general commandment thus reads: given a cultural object, we only know it adequately if we force ourselves to consider only those of its properties that are ultimately analyzable in terms of differential relations.

We are indeed dealing with minimal systems here, since properties are reduced to one unique type; we are thus dealing with entirely unspecified systems, since they can and must be able to apply to objects that are materially varied: phonemes, commodities, women.

Thesis 3 is much stronger than thesis 2. Perhaps linguists are the only ones to have made use of it. Combined with thesis 2 it means this: considered existentially (*an sit*), an element of a system only subsists as an element insofar as it is a term in a differential relation; if it is settled that it exists, then the question of the properties of its elements (*quid sit*) is raised, and it will only have as properties those that take part in a differential relation.

All the practitioners of structural linguistics know these propositions and hold them to be trivial. They are not. They amount to a reversal of the generally received relationship between properties and relations. In fact, ordinarily a being is given; properties are attributed to it (by sensory or perceptual or conceptual analysis, it doesn't matter which); it is then, and on this foundation, that we can conclude that with respect to another being, analyzed in a similar and independent manner, the two are in a relation of resemblance or difference (complete or partial).

Here, the approach is entirely different: difference is taken to be first, and it is what authorizes properties. This can only mean one thing: there is a differential relation that owes nothing to properties, since it precedes them. Moreover, this is indeed what a consistent structuralist linguist concludes: there are linguistic objects that are qualitatively similar and that count as two (in other words, Leibniz's principle of indiscernibility is rejected); there are qualitatively dissimilar linguistic objects that count as one. Thus, Benveniste maintained that the two Greek words *domos*, possessing the same phonic form and referring to the same signified thing (what we call a house), were linguistically two separate entities ("Homophonies radicales en indo-européen," Benveniste 1955, 21–22); conversely, reasoning by free variation posits that two phonetically dissimilar entities can be one from a linguistic point of view; in French, for example, the rolled r and the non-rolled r. Reasoning by contextual variation posits that the perceptible dissimilarity between the [m] in the English *pimp* and the [n] in the English *pint* does not affect the unity of these two nasals: the labial character of the first just repeats the labial character of the /p/ that follows it, and the dental character of the second just repeats the dental character of the /t/ that follows it; in fact, in this case there is only one single nasal entity, taking two dissimilar but not distinct forms, depending on the context; more technically, there is reasoning by complementary distribution: thus the *Ich-Laut* and the *Ach-Laut* in German count as a single phoneme, precisely because they are dissimilar to each other and not ever encountered in the same context.[18]

To say that /b/ is only voiced because it is different from /p/ is to say that the affirmation of their difference precedes the attribution of the property "voiced." And since, moreover, there are only properties on the basis of differences, this means that difference itself is disjoined from any property.

It is even disjoined from positive existence since, as Saussure notes, "language may be content simply to contrast something with nothing" (Saussure 1986 [1916], 86). Such that a negation of vocal material can be a term in a differential relation and can acquire properties on this foundation alone. This is the theory of the zero sign, which all structuralists, whether linguists or not, used; but only the linguists posited its elements. With the blissful ignorance of genius, Saussure had thus swept away with a wave of his hand an axiom that classical metaphysics took to be indispensable: "the nothing has no properties."[19] On the contrary, the nothing can have properties, and this is essential to the general notion of structure; Lacan recalls this in his theories of the subject and of desire (even if he does use the word *lack*, a term borrowed from discourses otherwise foreign to structure, as shorthand for a discursive rupture that is due to structure alone).

Structuralist linguistics thus makes use of what could be called *pure difference*. We see that it could not be the double of resemblance, contrary to the usual doctrine. In other words, structural linguistics is ignorant of the relation of resemblance: it has no use for it; it has at its disposal only a differential relation that is homonymous with what is usually called "difference," but which is separated from it, since it does not have an opposite.

3. The Seriousness of Structure

Lacan did not explicitly take a stand on methodological minimalism. He does not seem to have ever rejected it, although he never restricted himself to either the *more geometrico* or the order of reasons, even as strictly stylistic constraints. In any case, he never disavowed attempts—sporadic, it is true—to submit his teaching to the principles of demonstrative maximum and minimum. We can characterize his position as one of strict neutrality, if not indifference. So we will set the question aside.

Lacan did believe in object minimalism. The analogue of this is found in the appendix to the "Seminar on 'The Purloined Letter'" (Lacan 2006a, 33–46): it attempts to understand the unconscious as the functioning of a system to which the least possible number of properties are attributed. What appears then is that, by means of what are initially strictly differential terms (reducible to abstract entities, deprived of any property, and noted +/–) and barely specified operations (in fact, they reduce to aleatory occurrences and successions of such occurrences), regularities can be made to appear—lineaments, concretions . . . in short, a sort of structured and material landscape.

The term *chain* is given to a system that is at once an unspecified system and one reduced to its minimal properties: we should not understand this word in terms of concatenation, as a formal operation; nor in terms of one-dimensionality as such; it serves rather as an allusion, by the minimal character of its unique dimension, to system-minimalism. At the same time, dimensions like horizontality, verticality, and depth only play a figurative role.

So if "structure" is the term for an unspecified system as such, then "chain" is the term for minimal structure. This means that structuralism in linguistics can be put the following way: "we will know language (some particular natural language) only by forcing ourselves to consider it exclusively as a chain." Structural linguistics thus proves that a methodologically pure theory of the chain is at once possible and fruitful, and that this is even the case when it does not directly use the notion of a chain.

The term *signifier* is shorthand for the following: to not consider an unspecified element except in terms of the minimal properties that a system attributes to it, a system which itself is reduced to its minimal systemic properties; and to only consider an unspecified system from the point of view of the minimal elements into which it can be divided. This term, "signifier," is certainly taken from Saussure, but it parts ways with him since it is torn away from the symmetrical couple signifier/signified into which Saussure had placed it. It thus contains two divergent propositions: (1) that linguistics is reinterpreted, if not hijacked, and (2) that thanks to this reinterpretation, it is proven that on the basis of linguistics a structural analysis is legitimate for objects other than language.

There is no doubt that this is an intentional forcing on Lacan's part. Not all structuralist[20] linguists think that a chain is sufficient: they generally supplement it by organizing chains into strata: each stratum is certainly a chain, but there have to be several strata in order for the empirical dimension of languages to be grasped. For Lacan, by contrast, strata do not exist. In other words, linguistics is only decisive once it has been displaced. Its vocabulary is put to use, but in order to say something else.

This shows us why everything is interconnected in the concept of the signifying chain: signifiers exist only in a chain, and in order for a system to form a chain, it has to be constituted by signifiers.

Thus, Lacan believed in property minimalism. He even expressed his view on this in an especially explicit manner. When system is defined as structure, to hold that there are only properties that are induced by a system is to hold that every property is only the effect of structure. Thus, it is to hold that structure is causal. And when the element of every structure is defined as a signifier, this means that a signifier does not *have* properties, it *makes* them: it is action. This is how Lacan uses the grammatical letter of the Saussurean couple (perhaps taken from the Greek: *semainonta/semainomena*): "pure action of the signifier, pure passion of the signified"; this statement can be interpreted in terms of active and passive participles (see "The Signification of the Phallus," Lacan 2006i, 578).

Pure difference, which owes nothing to properties because, since it founds them, it is anterior to them, is what Lacan summarizes under the name of the Other. The capital letter, as well as the epithet "big" that sometimes precedes it, has led to many theologizing deviations.[21] The point, however, is different: it is the fact that one is dealing in this case with an other that is not the double of the same, that is neither its limit nor an opposed or particular case of it. This Other, without opposition, does not depend on property differences, since no property is attributed to it.[22] The fact that there is something like the Other is what makes it possible to posit one signifier and another, whereas as signifiers they are beyond the similar and dissimilar; this is also what the *factum linguae* establishes, since this *factum,* which structural linguistics once seemed to validate, depends on there being differences that precede properties. The Other is a guarantor, but it is not God; its guarantee boils down to this: if we could not say that there is an Other, there would not be speech. But, there is speech [*ça parle*].

Object minimalism and property minimalism put together make the *logion* "the unconscious is structured like a language" into a tautology. In fact a language, by hypothesis, has nothing but structural properties. But, again by hypothesis, these structural properties are necessarily minimal. But if they are minimal, everything structured will have them: therefore everything structured is necessarily structured like a language. In addition to being tautological, the *logion* also becomes contradictory because it seems to assume, by using the article *a,* that there are several *structurally* distinguishable languages: but if a language as language has only minimal properties, no language can be *structurally* distinguished from any other. The *logion* thus only states that the unconscious is structured. From this, there are only two options: either we are limited to repeating that the structuralist thesis is being adopted, and that we are limiting ourselves to the method that follows from it . . . in which case the *logion* has only a social significance (affirming one's membership in structuralism); or else we point out a determinate structural property that will be true of any unspecified structure, that will distinguish every structure, as such, from what is not a structure. . . . but that does not distinguish any structure from any other.

Perhaps alone among all the structuralists, Lacan consciously chose the second option. Perhaps he alone grasped its necessity. It amounts to admitting to what can be called the hyper-structural conjecture:

Any unspecified structure has some properties that are not unspecified.

Although it was never explicitly formalized, this conjecture takes us to the hard kernel of Lacanian doctrine. It is at the very foundation of some of its most important parts. More precisely still, it shows us that one of the fundamental goals of the doctrine can and must consist in the elaboration of a theory of unspecified structure as such.

One of the theorems of this theory is that, among the non-unspecified properties of an unspecified structure (insofar, at least, as it is considered uniquely as a structure and insofar as it is reduced to its minimal properties) is the emergence of the subject. Reciprocally, a necessary and sufficient condition for the construction of a theory of the subject is the enumeration of the properties that the unspecified structure confers upon it.

So, a provisional theorem:

The minimal unspecified structure contains, in an external inclusion, a certain distinct being that will be called the subject.

Since signifiers are nothing other than the minimal elements of any structure whatsoever, the definition of the signifier must include this emergence. Whence the *logion* "a signifier is what represents the subject to another signifier" ("The Subversion of the Subject and Dialectic of Desire in the Freudian Unconscious," Lacan 2006k, 694). This can be broken down into four defining theses:

1. A signifier only represents *to*;
2. That to which it represents can only be a signifier;
3. A signifier can only represent the subject;
4. The subject is only what a signifier represents to another signifier.

Theses 1 through 3, taken together, are nothing more and nothing less than a definition of the chain. This definition is entirely contained in the relation "X represents Y for Z." This relation, as we can see, is ternary; in this respect, it is distinguished from the classical relation of representation famously identified by Foucault (*The Order of Things*, 1973 [1966], 58–67), which is binary; it is equally distinguished from the Saussurean definition of signifiers, in which the relation of representation plays no role. The subject becomes an intrinsic property of the chain; this is thesis 4: every signifying chain, as such, includes the subject; but the subject itself has no other definition than to be the Y-term in a ternary relation in which X is a signifier and Z is another. The subject is second in relation to the signifier (Lacan, *Seminar XI*, 1978 [1973], 141).[23]

From the hyper-structural conjecture and the theory of unspecified structures thus follows a thesis that can be called the *hypothesis of the subject of signifiers*:

There is no subject but of some signifier.

If we admit the hypothesis of the subject of science in addition to this, the equation of subjects automatically follows:

> *The subject of science, the Cartesian subject, the Freudian subject, if they*
> *are subjects, can only be the subjects of some signifiers; they are, and*
> *can only be, one and the same.*

This conclusion is self-evident, but it can also be confirmed. The Cartesian subject can and must be established as the subject of some signifier: a necessary and sufficient condition for this to be the case is that the *cogito* be rewritten as a chain: *I think "therefore I am."*[24] The Freudian subject, the subject able to have an unconscious, can and must be established as the subject of some signifier: a necessary and sufficient condition for this to be the case is that the unconscious be conceived as a chain, which the *logion* "the unconscious, structured like a language" does. The subject of mathematized science can and must be established as the subject of some signifier: a necessary and sufficient condition for this to be the case is that mathematics be conceived as the signifier's eminent form, disjoined from any signified; and extended Galileism does this: the *logion* "the mathematics of the signifier" ("Science and Truth," Lacan 2006m, 731) is assumed to be appropriate for characterizing every science, and must be read in both directions—signifiers are intrinsically mathematical, and mathematics is intrinsically made of signifiers. In order for the Cartesian subject and the Freudian subject to be completely equated with each other, all that is needed is that there be a subject as soon as there is some thinking, even if it is impossible for the subject to state "therefore I am" ("C'est à la lecture de Freud . . ." ["Préface à l'ouvrage de Robert Georgin"] Lacan 1984 [1977], 14]); a necessary and sufficient condition for this to be the case is that the subject be nothing other than what incessantly emerges and disappears in a signifying chain. But this subject is also the subject without qualities required by science; the thought without qualities, whose correlate it is assumed to be, is able to receive positive expression in the non-unspecified laws of signifiers—laws without qualities, but also beyond quantity. The line of reasoning thus folds into itself, each part confirming the other.

In its initial form (chapter 2, pp. 21–24), the constitutive identity between the Cartesian and Freudian subjects was only partially demonstrated. The constitution appropriate to the subject of science, to which both were, separately, identified, was left obscure; all that was affirmed was that it was stripped of every quality, except for a thought that was itself stripped of any quality. But henceforth the theory of unspecified structure allows a positive thesis to be articulated. And this additional thesis is not historical; the equation of subjects no longer depends on a system of discursive conditions and successions. It is no longer necessary to assume that the emergence of the *cogito* allows for the emergence of the unconscious in a chronological chain of discourses. The correlation is structural.

4. Toward a Transcendental Reading

Under these conditions, two propositions can be extracted:

1. *The signifying chain is nothing less than the most general possible definition of thought, reduced to its minimal properties: in other words, signifiers are a thinking without qualities.*

2. *Reduced to its structural properties and stripped of qualities that are foreign to it (these include those of the soul), every metaphysical subject can be reinterpreted as the subject of signifiers. The hyper-structural conjecture thus issues a claim on metaphysics.*

In fact, the hyper-structural conjecture does allow itself to be read in a way that is homonymical to transcendental philosophy. The link is profound. Albert the Great called *transcendentia* those properties that belong to *every* object, as opposed to "ordinary" properties that only ever belong to a subset of objects which are able to be opposed to each other. More exactly, a property P is only well defined if it allows us to distinguish between the objects that have this property and those that do not. Transcendental properties are an exception to this, if they exist: every object has them, and they do not allow us to distinguish between one object and another; they belong to any object whatsoever. Albert the Great allowed that there were three such properties: the property of being *unum*, the property of being *verum*, and the property of being *bonum*.[25] So a theory was transcendental if it took one of these properties as its object. Kantian philosophy is indeed transcendental in this strict sense. But we see the result: to admit that there are "transcendental" properties that are neither indefinable nor empty is to admit that an unspecified object as such has non-unspecified properties.

A transcendental method would consist of stripping an object of its particular properties, doing so in the most systematic manner possible, and nevertheless succeeding in discovering that, despite having been stripped down, just before it ceases to be thinkable at all, the object turns out to be neither completely empty nor completely without structure. The properties left over cannot be otherwise than they are because, if it happened to be the case that they were different, the object would cease to be, or to be thinkable. The properties are not affected by diversity, since they are obtained by the elimination of diversity. However, since they allow us to grasp the minimum conditions under which an object is or is thinkable, they also allow us to grasp what it is that allows the diverse to be or to be thinkable.

Obviously Lacan does not adopt Albert the Great's list of transcendental properties; we could even say that he contradicts it point by point. The doctrine of the signifier attests to this. Sticking to the letter of Saussure, the being of one signifier among others is only sustained by the multiplicity of all the others; this is the most direct consequence of the definition in terms of differences alone. The *ens* here is not an *unum*. As for the arbitrariness that is supposed to govern the relationship between the signifier and the signified, its exact nature is hardly important (it was up for debate as much by linguists as by Lacan); one thing in any case is certain: arbitrariness eliminates any pertinence the Good and the True might have for the signifier. In this respect, the Lacanian definition of the signifier just accentuates the Saussurean rupture: a signifier, as a mode of being, for Saussure as for Lacan, is neither one, nor good, nor true, in the sense in which the philosophical tradition has understood these, and yet, it does not cease to be.

However, a doubt arises. That Lacan systematically denies the transcendental properties inherited by the tradition is certain; but is it certain that he allows that there are properties of this type even if they are different from the tradition's properties? I would not say so. Nevertheless, the analogy between the transcendental properties of the unspecified object and the minimal properties of the unspecified system is striking. If philosophical language is used—Lacan did not repudiate it at the time—this analogy becomes a homonymy; it redoubles and confirms the homonymy found in the axiom of the subject (chapter 2, p. 17). It could be argued that the *Cahiers pour l'Analyse* project was based on this double homonymy; more exactly, that it aimed to turn it into a synonymy. The research program could be put this way:

> *The hypothesis of the subject of signifiers is not just any consequence of the hyper-structural conjecture: it is its major consequence.*

or:

> *The hyper-structural conjecture is the modern form of the transcendental question.*

It also says:

The subject of signifiers is the modern metaphysical subject.

And finally, it says:

What can and must a modern metaphysics be?

Modern in this sense: just as Kant incorporated Galilean science (in its Newtonian version), the metaphysics entailed by the hyper-structural conjecture would incorporate the new Galileism, of which Lacan is simultaneously the demonstration and the herald. Just as Kant wrote the *First Principles of a Metaphysics of Science and Nature* [in English, this work is known as *Metaphysical Foundations of Natural Science*], we could imagine someone writing the "First Principles of Analysis," in which analysis would designate what psychoanalysis, extended Galileism, and the metaphysics implied by it have in common. Its preferred method is the theory of the signifier, inasmuch as (1) signifiers are nothing else but the unspecified elements of unspecified structure, (2) according to the hyper-structural conjecture, signifiers are assumed to be the bearers of non-unspecified properties, and (3) according to the theory of the subject, these non-unspecified properties include the emergence of a distinct element able to be called the subject. Among the established disciplines, the most appropriate are those that purify their object of any substance and that, methodologically, respect the laws of an axiomatic minimalism; in other words, logic. Whence the fact that the phrase *logic of the signifier* is given to the theory of the signifier.

This logic includes both mathematical logic and formal ontology—Platonic, Neoplatonic, Fichtean. The intended outcome: to generate in an axiomatic manner (while respecting method minimalism) the exhaustive list of minimal non-unspecified properties of unspecified signifiers.

It should not be a surprise that the transcendental program and the minimalist program are stitched together. Of course, the minimalism of the structuralists was often a phenomenalism, connected to a resolute empiricism (this is Martinet's position), but we know that it is not at all impossible to go from phenomenalism to transcendental idealism. Moreover, there is a strong link between empiricist minimalism and metaphysical minimalism: to assume nothing about an object beyond what is necessary in order to be able to describe it empirically; to assume nothing about an object beyond what is necessary in order to think it; and to discover that by stripping an object of its properties, one is not left with a void but rather with an irreducibly subsisting rock of non-unspecified properties.

Lacan did not formulate the program of the *Cahiers pour l'Analyse,* he did not adopt it as his own, but he did not disavow it either (see "Discourse à l'École freudienne de Paris," Lacan 2001c [1970], 268). Consequently, we can take this to be a giveaway: we can recognize in the program, in a riskier and, because of this, more readable form, some important properties of what I will henceforth call *the first Lacanian classicism.*

The great masterpiece of this classicism is the *Écrits,* taken in its entirety, minus the texts that are explicitly presented as "antecedents" (in section 2). This work constitutes the progressive and almost systematic development of the program articulated in the Rome Discourse in 1953. It bases the hyper-structural thesis on the assumed evidence of structuralisms, which are taken to be contemporary forms of a new Galileism that is itself considered an extension of strict Galileism; this extension maintains or, more exactly, purifies the equation of subjects and the hypothesis of the subject of science that is its linchpin. Its constituent parts are now clear:

> Science's Core Doctrine specifically includes the hypothesis of the subject of science;
>
> The Galileism invoked in the Core Doctrine takes on a particular form that is founded on an extension of the notion of mathematization and an extension of its universe to nonnatural objects: this is extended Galileism;
>
> Extended Galileism includes psychoanalysis, thanks to the *logion* "the unconscious is structured like a language"; but this *logion* itself requires the hyper-structural conjecture;
>
> The hyper-structural conjecture, as a theory of unspecified structure, and insofar as it is a theory that includes the emergence of the subject, is a way to resolve the hypothesis of the subject of science; consequently, it hinges on the axiom of the subject, homonymous and possibly synonymous with that of classical metaphysics.

This edifice was majestic. We understand why, presenting itself to our gaze in the form of a book, it had the force of an oeuvre. However, it was not destined to extend and elaborate itself with new additions that would complete the floor plan: its fate was to be overturned. Certain events[26] did play a role in these adventures, but only the intrinsic causes were decisive: as majestic as it was, the edifice was unstable.

4

The Second Lacanian Classicism

1. The Instabilities of the First Classicism

If the first classicism is not stable, it is due to how it understands science's Core Doctrine. The problem is easy to diagnose.

—Instability due to historicism: science's Core Doctrine, by its internal logic, is not historicizing; the existence of a theory of the subject testifies to this. But in 1966 the implications had not been drawn out. The version that the *Écrits* gives is expressed in terms of inaugural emergence, succession, and contemporaneity; it makes use of historians' notions, even if it is more and more overtly just a matter of a historicizing style, and even if nothing substantial depends on it anymore. In this respect, the first classicism is out of sync with itself; the theory of the break and the theory of the subject do not go together.[1]

—Instability due to the concept of mathematization. Mathematization must be understood in terms of nonquantitative literalization. We have already said that the evolution of mathematics itself allows for this: especially Bourbakism.[2] But Bourbakism is only one figure in a more general movement dedicated to reconstructing the entirety of mathematics on secure logical foundations. In other words, Bourbakism affirms three things about mathematics: (1) it is autonomous with respect to Galilean science; (2) its essence is not quantitative; it can thus be extended to nonquantitative objects; and (3) there is a mathematical logic. But Koyré assumes exactly the opposite: (1') whatever it is in itself, mathematics is only considered the servant of mathematization; (2') it is to be taken only in the narrow sense of quantity, which, according to Koyré, is the only thing modern science is interested in; and (3') there is no mathematical logic (see "The Liar," Koyré 1946).

Affirmation 3' can certainly be considered idiosyncratic and superfluous to the theses on physics. (I myself do not believe this particular affirmation at all, but that's not important.) It remains the case that by admitting even the legitimacy of mathematical logic, a consistent follower of Koyré holds that its mathematicity is not at all important for the mathematization at work in science. In short, science's Core Doctrine, reduced to its foundations, cannot accord the least importance to mathematical logic in particular and to the axiomatization of mathematics in general.

But this is a position that the first Lacanian classicism, in its completed form, cannot hold, because of its extended Galileism, as we have said: it is important that mathematics be literal and not quantitative, and only axiomatization allows for this. And equally because of the theory of unspecified structure, in which it is assumed that mathematical logic plays a determining role. The first classicism needs mathematical logic: both its general existence and some of its particular propositions (for example, Gödel's theorem). It also needs science's Core Doctrine. But the two paths diverge as soon as one of them is followed consistently enough.

—An instability due to the contradiction between the ideal science of structuralism, which is born of Greek *epistèmè*, and the Core Doctrine's ideal of science, which rejects this same *epistèmè*. This contradiction intensifies if science's Core Doctrine is interpreted in a non-historicizing manner; then, in fact, the synonymy between Koyré's distinguishing feature and Popper's becomes decisive. But Popper's distinguishing feature is directly opposed to the ancient axiomatic and to any axiom of the minimum. The paradox is that the non-historicizing reading is induced by structuralism by itself.

—Instability due to a lack of precision regarding the concept of the letter. This is constitutive for extended Galileism; it alone is what allows for a smooth transition from mathematics to the sciences of culture, and from them to psychoanalysis. But it does not become the object of a theory that is autonomous relative to the theory of the signifier. The canonical text for this point of view is "The Instance of the Letter," which states the two separately, but also puts them into a reciprocal correlation (Lacan 2006f). Because of this, many of the propositions formulated about letters and literality seem just as well to be about signifiers, and vice versa. If minimalism is taken seriously, this equivalence should have made one of the two theories redundant. If, however, there is not any redundancy, it must be because the correlation's reciprocity falls apart. But no such failure ever emerges. In the absence of a decision on this point, the concepts of the letter and the signifier both become obscure; neither the signifying property nor the literal property of mathematics is able to attain an entirely clear status. At the same time, to affirm that mathematization is literalization is neither clear nor distinct.

—Instability due to the evolution of linguistics. At the time of the Rome Discourse, it seemed to be a completed science, in the two senses of the word: both finished and sterile. Lacan considers linguistics both methodologically exemplary and unable to teach him anything new, compared to its golden age in Geneva, Moscow, and Prague ("Radiophonie" speaks of the "failure of the linguist" regarding the foundation of the journal *La Psychanalyse* in 1953 [Lacan 2001e, 410]). This double belief, concealed by relations of esteem or friendship for Benveniste or Jakobson, is nevertheless characteristic of the first classicism: linguistics plays the role of a guarantor, but this is because of its past contributions; there is nothing to expect from it anymore.

But two events occur, each the opposite of the other. On the one hand there was the discovery of Saussure's anagrams (in 1964) and, even more importantly, the consequences of this discovery for Jakobson: he thought he would be able to found an entirely new poetics, in linguistic terms, on its basis, worthy in his eyes of being ranked among the great innovations of the twentieth century. On the other hand was the emergence of Chomsky starting in the 1960s; this proved that structural linguistics was not a completed science, that there were other paths that a Galileism in linguistic matters could follow; that once again a science of language was possible. But, at the same time, everything was overturned.

Because while the anagrams and the poetics turned out to be important for psychoanalysis, they contained something foreign to any extended Galileism. As for Chomsky, he allied himself to Galileism, but to a non-extended version of it, which over time led to a re-naturalization of language (see the theme of the organ, commented on in the session of December 9, 1975, of Seminar XXIII (Lacan 2016 [2005], 21). Not only is there nothing in his method concerning signifiers anymore, nor the chain, nor unspecified structure . . . but whatever is new about his method does not add anything to Baconism, and nothing that it says about language is compatible with the *fact* of psychoanalysis. If this is the case, a turn towards the natural sciences would be just as fruitful.

Extended Galileism could not withstand these multiple instabilities. We could say that by 1970 the transformation is to a great extent already underway. A second phase begins. I will call it the *second Lacanian classicism.*

Its program was never completely put forward. In the 1970s there is nothing equivalent to the Rome Discourse, although in Seminar XX we find here and there some exciting hints. Taking the first classicism as our starting point we can, however, detect the displacements, suppressions, and additions which altogether turn out to be coherent and sketch out the new configuration.

If science's Core Doctrine is to continue to be pertinent for psychoanalysis, in the absence of an extended Galileism it has to be reformulated. We can even say that, in a paradox we could well call dialectical, the obvious end of structuralism made explicit the anti-historicism that structuralism led to during the time of its greatest power. In 1953 (before its excessive spread began, denounced in 1965) structuralism, or rather its premises, was able to pass itself off as the datable emergence of a new form of modern science. In historicizing readings one could easily believe that history was being made: 1945 was not so far away. But by 1968 structuralism was already no more; the emergence had been a false emergence. Let's add that apparently Lacan had concluded from the barricades that History, truly, did not exist (or did not any longer). Whence his skepticism not about the modern, but about chronological readings of it.

To the precise extent that the Core Doctrine is at one and the same time purified of historicism and stripped of extended Galileism, it has just one foundation left: literalization. An autonomous theory of letters thus becomes not only desirable but essential. It will lead to changes in the theory of mathematics. Bourbaki had established the synonymy between literalization and mathematization: initially it let the first be clarified by the second; it turns out that the second can, for its part, also be clarified by the first.

If the hyper-structural conjecture has to be maintained, it will be in the paradoxical situation of no longer being able to base itself on the structuralist movement. Even more than before, Lacan's doctrine has to rely on its own resources for developing the theory of unspecified structures and the theory of pure difference separated from every qualitative property. As conceptual as their formulation is, these two theories are no longer able to engage with the transcendental; only structuralism authorized the homonymy between the minimalisms; in its absence, object minimalism and property minimalism have no faith in modern metaphysics. So this means that the synonymical reading of the axiom of the subject loses its depth; and the axiom itself loses its importance if it is limited to homonymy. The second classicism, in contrast to the first, can let itself be indifferent toward philosophy.

Linguistics, too, will cease to matter. All that remains are a select few of its practitioners. Lacan will treat them as prized witnesses not to a science but to an art, who encounter the flaws of the subject in the material they deal with—their own flaws, in fact. As for Jakobson, the master of languages, the linguist in him will give way to the poet; and Lacan, unlike Jakobson, does not think that they are the same. Consequently, Stalin's theorem will be thrown into the dustbin. From then on what is important is to make a mark on language, to make it suddenly different from how it had been before. Mayakovsky instead of Stalin, and Joyce above all. Politicians and scholars have said that revolution never changes language; but revolution or not, some subject, sometimes, changes language, Lacan will soon say.

We can say that the totality of the *Scripta* after 1968 belongs to this program, notwithstanding some transitional retrospective writings (like "Radiophonie") or prospective ones (like the last sessions of Seminar XX). Despite the absence of a synthetic exposition, the program was nevertheless implemented [*mise en oeuvre*].

2. The Matheme

The second classicism's pivot point is the concept of the matheme. It alone is what lets the propositions about science's Core Doctrine, letters, mathematics, and philosophy be joined together. It was developed by Lacan beginning in 1972. The principal sources for it are "L'Étourdit" (Lacan 2001f [1972], 449–95) and Seminar XX.

Some quotes will allow us to begin our examination: "this language of the pure matheme, by which I mean that alone which is able to teach" ("L'Étourdit," 472); "The matheme is declared from the only real that is recognized at first in language: namely, number" (ibid., 481); "a speaking such as mine . . . becomes . . . teachable only after I have mathematized it, along Meno-like lines" (482–83); "I made the unteachable into a matheme, in order to provide it with the fixion of true opinion, fixion written with an x, but not without the resources of equivocation" (483); "Mathematical formalization is our goal, our ideal. Why? Because it alone is matheme, in other words, it alone is capable of being integrally transmitted" (*Seminar XX*, Lacan 1998 [1975], 119).

We should distinguish right away between two questions: the specific question of the matheme, of its function and its form, and the general question of mathematics and its status. These two questions intersect, since the concept of the matheme is based on a thesis about mathematics, and since every particular matheme is a specified fragment selected from the totality of mathematical writings (not without occasional alterations). But the distinction remains: there are in Lacan references to mathematics that do not depend on the doctrine of the matheme. Even if this is only for a chronological reason: the *Écrits* precede "L'Étourdit" by six years. The chronology is, moreover, augmented by structural differences. In other words, the appearance of an explicit doctrine on the matheme modified Lacan's relationship to mathematics, and, by virtue of this, to mathematization. This affects the very heart of science's Core Doctrine.

2.1. Function and Form of the Matheme

For Lacan, the matheme's function and form are determined by two affirmations:

> *(a) The matheme assures the complete transmissibility of knowledge;*
> *(b) The matheme conforms to the mathematical paradigm.*

Proposition (b), if we strictly adhere to the terms in which it is articulated, implies the following: the matheme will be to mathematics what the phoneme is to phonetics: a unit of knowledge, just as the other is a unit of sound. Reciprocally, mathematics will be to the matheme what phonetics is to the phoneme: a theory of the general conditions for well-formed mathemes, as the other is a theory of the general conditions for well-formed phonemes. This assumes that phonetics is able to define what it is to be a phoneme as such; similarly, this assumes that mathematics is able to define what mathematicity is as such.

In order to understand the significance of proposition (a), we have to contend with the fact that complete transmissibility presents us with an issue that goes back to science's Core Doctrine.

For a long time it was assumed that a necessary part of the transmission of knowledge, or at least of its complete transmission, was the intervention of a subject for whom there was no replacement—a master, who dispensed a surplus knowledge to his disciples both by his Spoken Word (one form of which could be silence) and his Presence (one form of which could be absence). Without this surplus knowledge, which is called wisdom and which should inspire a form of love, and without the master who was its support, no complete transmission could occur. This ancient arrangement, which was connected to *epistèmè*, can be recognized here.

This is precisely what the doctrine of the matheme rules out: if we cannot say that this is a necessary consequence of science's Core Doctrine, it is clear at any rate that it is required as its condition *sine qua non*. To affirm (a) is in fact to affirm propositions of the following type:

There are no masters,

or:

There are no disciples,

or:

There is no wisdom,

or:

There is neither Spoken Word nor Presence,

or:

There is no wisdom beyond knowledge.

These exclusions characterize the modern universe. We can see this better if (a) and (b) are combined, which gives us the subjacent thesis:

Mathematics is the paradigm of complete transmissibility.

If the way modern science is transmitted does not require masters (but at the very most, professors), it is precisely because it puts all its confidence in the literal functioning of mathematics. Reciprocally, if modern science puts all its confidence in the literal functioning of mathematics, this implies that it is not wisdom (a scandal that ethics committees and churches are eager to expose). This also implies that, in the universe of science, there is no master or, what amounts to the same thing, that the word "master" just designates a position.

According to Stalin's theorem, languages do not change even when the infrastructure does; so from the ancient world to the modern universe the term "master" persists, but only as a homonym. The ancient master was the master in the sense of someone for whom there was no replacement, and he remained so beyond his position in the social network; his individual attributes (his virtues) were essential for qualifying him positively (Socrates, such as the oracle at Delphi had determined him). The modern master is only a master because he occupies a position, one in which he is infinitely replaceable by anyone else, and his individual attributes are inessential and fundamentally negative; it suffices that they do not disqualify him.

From this, among other things, follow certain traits of normal science that otherwise seem to be anecdotal. Such as the precarious status of proper names: they are only allowed into it as stand-ins for the propositions attributed to them; in no case do they indicate someone for whom there is no replacement. Thus the slow, but ineluctable, absorption of science by the university: in the university every scholar is able to be replaced by another, but by virtue of this fact he is homomorphic to the professor. Thus the rise in the importance of the professor, who is committed to transmission (literalized when it comes to science, not necessarily literalized when it comes to other disciplines); as long as an individual, put in the position of an instrument of transmission, correctly performs his function, none of his personal characteristics will be taken to be virtues except those that, by their transparency and their innocuousness, do not prevent him from functioning well; for this reason he is easily replaceable. Dullness, drab colors, mild-mannered behaviors, these are what are expected when everything is a matter of position, not (of) subject.[3] How much of this holds true for science in the making, the science of breaks and revolutions, is obviously another matter, but we are not talking about that.

In Lacan's case, the doctrine of the matheme is thus linked to a doctrine in which the master is a purely positional determination. This alone is compatible with science's Core Doctrine; it is put forward in the theory of the four discourses, in which the distinction between terms and positions is completely worked out.[4] But, sticking to the *via negativa*, the absence of the ancient figure of the master was already implicit in the "return to Freud." Such a slogan is based on a hidden thesis: if there has to be a return to Freud in order for the true object of psychoanalysis to be grasped, this implies that something about psychoanalysis is immune to the difference between German and French. Strictly speaking, it is not a matter of good or bad translations; to be more precise, Freud can be translated better than he has been, but in the absence of a suitable translation we can, by means of commentary and interpretation, do without one (we see here, apart from the anecdotes, what separates Lacan from Laplanche).[5] The thesis is all the more striking since, in addition, it holds that the object of psychoanalysis is thoroughly traversed not only by language, but by languages; however, this does not prevent it from being the case that in going from Freud, speaking and thinking in German, to Lacan, speaking and thinking in French, a complete transmission is possible.

The battle against the International Psychoanalytic Association (the first at least, directed at the London International and its familial *establishment*;[6] the second battle, directed at the U.S. International, is of another nature) enlarged the claim: since Freud is not a master (although he occupies the position of one), participation in his Presence and his Word does not give anyone any authority. So, Melanie Klein can prevail over Anna Freud. Likewise Lacan, who never met Freud, can prevail over Marie Bonaparte, who was on familiar terms with Freud. When, in the form of the matheme, letters became necessary and sufficient for transmission, the master/disciple couple, with its procession of fidelities and betrayals, is no more; the only pairings are literal: "Marx and Lenin, Freud and Lacan, are not coupled in being. It is via the letter they found in the Other that, as beings of knowledge, they proceed two by two" (*Seminar XX*, Lacan 1998 [1975], 97).

We can advance the thesis that the status of the École [Freudienne de Paris] hinges on the matheme, and the master's strictly positional determination. The École [Freudienne] is nothing other than the matheme's institutional correlate, and its main duty consists in assuring complete transmission. Thus the École expresses itself in a journal of mathemes, entitled *Scilicet* (which can be glossed: "you can know," *scil.* "thanks to the matheme"). In this journal, the relevance of Bourbaki's rhetorical model is striking: its anonymous texts. With one exception (Bourbaki's name in one, Lacan's in the other), this anonymity-minus-one testifies to an "intellectual collective" for which one name—it doesn't matter if the referent is fictitious or not—serves as the principle of its assembly. Far from being a flirtation, as the Hegelianism of *Capital* was according to Marx, the imitation of Bourbaki verifies the hold that mathematics has on the transmission of knowledge in the Freudian School. In fact, this singular format indicates a project: to rewrite psychoanalysis "mathematically" just as Bourbaki aimed to rewrite mathematics "mathematically." That the name "School" was chosen over the name "Society" or "Institute" is thus due to a nontrivial core doctrinal principle.[7]

"I am not a master, I just occupy the place of one": these are the conclusions that Lacan could not avoid drawing for himself when the configuration of his mathematization was most fully deployed. The following pun should be related to this thesis: "read Salomon, he's the master of masters, the master of feeling [*senti-maître*], someone of my own ilk" (*Seminar XX*, Lacan 1998 [1975], 115), in which one can hear the signifier "*antimaître*" [anti-master], a strict analogue to anti-philosophy.[8]

Especially since for such a long time there has been a deep connection between philosophy and mastery.

2.2. Letters

Why is mathematics the paradigm for transmissibility? As we have said, it is because of letters.

Now, letters are not signifiers. The distinction between them was not clear in the first classicism (see especially "The Instance of the Letter," Lacan 2006f); but it is accentuated and perfected through the course of the second classicism (see especially *Seminar XX*, Lacan 1998 [1975]). Here are its principal elements.

A signifier is only a relation: it represents *for* and it is that for which there is representation; letters certainly relate to other letters, but they are not only relational. Being only a differential relation, a signifier is without positivity; but a letter is positive. Differences among signifiers being prior to any quality, signifiers are without qualities; letters are qualified (they have a physiognomy, a sensible support, a reference, etc.). Signifiers are not identical to themselves, since there is no self to which they can be connected; but letters, whatever discourse they occur in, are identical to themselves. Signifiers being completely defined by their place in a system, it is impossible for them to be displaced; but it is possible to displace letters; thus the operation with letters par excellence involves permutation (witness the theory of four discourses). For the same reason, signifiers cannot be destroyed: at most a signifier can "lack in its place"; but letters, with their qualities and their identity, can be erased, effaced, abolished.[9] No one can clasp his hand around *a* signifier, since it exists only by an *other* signifier; but letters are able to be handled, if not grabbed (as Lacan remarks about the formula for universal gravitation, "this writing . . . summarized in these five little letters that can be written in the palm of your hand" [*Seminar XX*, Lacan 1998 (1975), 43]). Being displaceable and graspable, letters are transmissible; by their transmissibility, they transmit that of which they are the support, at the heart of a discourse; a signifier does not transmit itself and transmits nothing; it represents the subject for another signifier in the chain in which it is encountered. Signifiers are not instituted; whether they are called arbitrary (Saussure) or contingent (Lacan), these are certainly not the same thing, but it hardly matters for what they both agree on: namely, that signifiers do not have any reason to be as they are, first and foremost because a signifier is not *as* it is: because it has no self-identity; because it does not have a self; because every self is reflexive, and the signifier cannot be reflexive without being secondary to itself and another signifier. Letters, on the contrary, always belong to a declaration; in this sense they always have a reason to be as they are, even if this reason is just a pure and simple decision; this is why they always issue forth from a discourse ("The letter is, radically speaking, an effect of discourse" [*Seminar XX*, Lacan 1998 (1975), 36]); they are nothing without the rules that limit their use, but given these rules each letter is what it is, as it is; reflexivity is permissible for it; it has a self. These rules of use can be articulated ("what is written . . . only subsists if I employ, in presenting it, the language [*langue*] I make use of" (ibid., 119); the one who articulates them by that very fact occupies the position of a master in the game of letters, if not that of an inventor: Palamedes or Cadmus, Claude or St. Cyril. There is no master of signifiers. There is no inventor of them (except God, if that kind of thing exists).

In technical terms, the signifier is just S; but the letter knots together R, S, and I, which are heterogeneous to each other. Thus, everything about signifiers is said in terms of chains and alterities; reduced to their essence, signifiers are just S1 (a signifier), S2 (another signifier); $ (the subject barred by the alternation between S1 and S2); and *a* (which falls away under the effect of the bar).[10] But everything about letters is said in a vocabulary of encounters, obstructions, contacts, and in-betweenness. These vocabularies are multiple: the geometry of the line, topology, and logical quantification were all able to be used. They especially helped to develop the doctrine of the matheme, precisely insofar as the matheme falls under the letter's authority.

We can then see why Lacan talks about an *orthe doxa*; at least, we can understand this if the concept of *orthe doxa* is taken back to its Platonic origins (*The Republic*, 476c–478d; *Meno*, 97b–99b). For Plato, it was about drawing an intermediary segment on a line between two heterogeneities: *agnosia* and *epistème*. The *cross-cap* in "L'Étourdit" (Lacan 2001f [1972], 471) is a topological version of Plato's linear geometry—nonlinear and dramatic: stitch together two heterogeneities, a spherical part and an aspherical part, a cut on a Möbius strip. There is a logical version of an analogous clash: these are the paradoxes of the Whole, in which the doctrine of sexuation is written. Two lines run into each other here: one of them highlights, in a symbolism inspired by Russell, the structure of the Whole as limited, combining two paired propositions: one can only say "for every x, Φx" if one can also say "there is an x such that non-Φ-x"; the other one highlights, in anti-Russellian symbolism, the structure of the unlimited, for which the term Whole is not appropriate. If one must say "there is no x such that non-Φ-x," then the name of the whole must be barred: "for not-all x, Φ-x." The matheme does not consist in any one of these propositions taken in isolation, nor in any of the pairs taken in isolation, but in the confrontation between the two irreconcilable pairs.[11]

The most general model of the matheme is formed in this way, allowing us to see the necessity of heterogeneity in the sexual calculus, but also to see that the possibility and the necessity of the matheme in general are due to the fact that the speaking being is sexed.

Regarding *orthe doxa*, however, there is more to uncover than a clash between heterogeneous elements. Plato, let us recall, used the concept of being tethered to oppose *epistèmè* to *orthe doxa*: "that is why knowledge is something more valuable than right opinion. What distinguishes one from the other is the tether" (*Meno*, 98a).

But what characterizes the mathemes of psychoanalysis is the fact that they are not tethered to each other. Not only does each one of them stitch the heterogeneous together, but each one is in addition heteromorphic to the others. The writing they are made up of varies. There is no literal passage from one to the other: it is impossible to calculate a matheme on the basis of another simply by manipulating letters. The permutation that structures the theory of the four discourses is internal to one single matheme: the one that constitutes the four formulas taken together, and the rule that makes one change into the other. None of the four lines of the sexual matheme is obtained by any transformation of any of the others; they function all at the same time. There is no literal transition from one of these mathemes to the other. In short, the mathemes cannot be gathered together into a scientific corpus.

The following conclusion imposes itself: with the matheme, Lacan takes on everything about the mathematical paradigm except, precisely, deduction. The matheme is meant to be a local calculus; we can certainly draw from it all the propositions that it authorizes by manipulating its letters, but only those can be drawn, and no others. It being admitted, moreover, that no matheme can be drawn from any other matheme, these new propositions are nothing but nonmathematical and purely descriptive: a Lacanian matheme, insofar as it is literal, functions ideally as a matrix for the production of empirical propositions. One can and must draw from it only sublunar contingencies.[12]

The matheme states the formal hold of mathematics over psychoanalysis, but from mathematics it keeps only literality, disconnected from any arrangement into a line of reasoning. Or, to be more precise, the local calculus—the indivisible fragment of knowledge—that letters allow for (*litterâ scire licet*) is only permissible due to the silence the letter imposes on lines of reasoning.[13]

3. Mathematics

The doctrine of the matheme, as new as it was, turns out to depend on a trait common to all of Lacan's numerous and various borrowings from the realm of mathematical letters. What Lacan catches hold of in these letters is what they express regarding the suspensive, that is to say, the impossible: inaccessible infinity, the theory of number that is traversed by the incessant fissure of zero, and topology as a theory of a "no-space," tearing geometry away from any transcendental aesthetic.

If we group these borrowings together and reduce them to what they have in common, we get the definition of mathematics as the science of the real, insofar as the real names the function of the impossible (*Seminar XX*, Lacan 1998 [1975], 131). Of course, Gödel's theorem will often be cited in this context, but notice that Lacan's use of it is not original. He is content with finding in it what everyone finds in it: the rigorous demonstration that undecidable propositions exist in arithmetic. Much more structural is his reference to intuitionism. Compelled to only allow into mathematics what can be intuited as the product of a positive construction, Lacan is not so much hanging on to the doctrine of intuition as he is rejecting apagogic demonstration.[14] The stakes of this are enormous, since philosophers of mathematics, especially the most recent and one of the greatest among them, have held that the legitimacy of apagogical reasoning is at the very essence of mathematical deduction itself.[15] But Lacan's rejection can be easily explained: apagogical reasoning fundamentally depends on the tethering together of lines of reasoning, and such arrangements are proper to the imaginary.

Mathematics disjoined from deduction and the apagogic, reduced only to its letters . . . this is what is actually at work in the scattered and multiple references to mathematics; this is what the matheme lets us see in a completely explicit manner; moreover, this is what really does seem to constitute, in Lacan's eyes, the pertinence of mathematics for modern science.

For the second Lacanian classicism did not renounce Galileo at all. Quite to the contrary, it reaffirms science's Core Doctrine. Except, however, the mathematics implicated in its mathematization is entirely purified of whatever it might still contain of Euclid and the *more geometrico*. It has become profoundly un-Greek. Mathematics is important not because of how it chains together lines of reasoning, but because of the strictly circumscribed zones of literality that it authorizes—what we can call a "calculus."

We should not be afraid of articulating some radical propositions here. The doctrine of the matheme does not only allow Lacan to reaffirm the mathematizing move; in fact, it clarifies the foundations of science's Core Doctrine, showing them as they must be in order for psychoanalysis to depend on them. It is undeniable that the matheme of psychoanalysis is fragmented, local, and limited to a few letters. But in this respect it is no different from what is at work in the mathematization called for since Galileo. Quite to the contrary, it brings it to light in the harshest of manners.

In this light, it seems that modern science calls upon mathematics in its entirety, but rids it of what was most precious about it in the eyes of mathematicians who were faithful to their heritage: not only the *more geometrico*, but demonstration and any manner of tethering things together. Measure itself is only a leftover. From then on, the only thing that functions is calculus: "what does it mean when we write that inertia is $\frac{mv^2}{2}$ if not that, whatever the number of ones you place under each of those letters, you are subject to a certain number of laws—laws of grouping, addition, multiplication, etc." (*Seminar XX*, Lacan 1998 [1975], 130) This means: to all the regional laws of a particular type of calculus, but also only to those.

We find here, in a new form, the dividing line that separates *epistèmè* from science.

In *epistèmè* tethering things together is decisive—this is what Plato says explicitly; it is all the more so the less it is localized, and reasoning in a general form is the only thing that allows it to avoid depending on a particular location. It is thus important that a particular science be able to establish the general forms of reasoning, whether it is called a dialectic or a logic. Euclidean conventions give us an illustration of these general forms that is the most purified of any cluttering substances. The words "long chains of reasoning" are to be taken literally: a vast expanse of propositions, continuously tethered together.

In science, let's dare to say that tethering is not important, nor is demonstration by reasoning, but rather calculus, which is local (even when its locale turns out to be rather expansive). Calculus operates on letters, fixed by a discourse and combined according to rules that can be made explicit, in such a way as to produce a new literal combination; but these rules hold for only a given type of calculus. The Lacanian mathematization of psychoanalysis just takes one further step in this respect: calculus with letters moves so strongly away from any type of deduction, its locale is defined so restrictively, that its efficacy is limited only to the fragment of writing in which it can be read.

But does this not amount to a negation of mathematics? Apparently, the majority of mathematicians and the entirety of the philosophical tradition would say that it does; but Lacan parts ways with them. Not only does he affirm that his use of mathematics is legitimate and able to authorize a mathematization, he affirms even more: that this use exposes the very essence of mathematicity. With the matheme he proposes a new and scandalous definition of mathematicity as such, of what makes it the case that mathematics is mathematics. This definition relies on an *intrinsically* local character, coming from letters.

Lacan thinks his doctrine is strengthened by what is most cutting-edge about the Bourbaki project. In fact, by the program such as it is stated in the "Introduction" to book 1 of the *Elements of Mathematics*, and the procedures used in its first chapter. We have pointed out the rhetorical importance of Bourbaki for how *Scilicet* was formatted. It is time to point out a more substantial importance: the doctrine of the matheme only holds if we sign on to the Bourbakist interpretation of mathematics. Or, at least, to the entirely literalizing[16] interpretation that Lacan gives to the Bourbaki program: a mathematics founded on calculus (insofar as calculus is not deduction) and on letters (insofar as letters are not signs):

> Let us put together objects. . . . Let us assemble these absolutely heterogeneous things, and let us grant to ourselves the right to designate the resulting assemblage by a letter. That is how set theory expresses itself at the outset, that theory, for example, that I mentioned last time in relation to Nicolas Bourbaki.
>
> You have let slip by the fact that I said that the letter designates an assemblage. That is what is printed in the text of the definitive edition. . . . [The authors] are very careful to say that letters designate assemblages. Therein lies their timidity and their error—letters *constitute* [*font*] assemblages. They don't *designate* assemblages, they *are* assemblages. They are taken as [*comme*] functioning like [*comme*] these assemblages themselves. (*Seminar XX*, Lacan 1998 [1975], 47–48)

According to Lacan, Bourbaki in fact is still not Bourbakist enough. Moreover, we know that Bourbaki uses deduction as well as apagogics. And moreover, he affirms the seamless continuity of mathematical demonstration since the Greeks: "what constituted a proof for Euclid is still a proof for us" (Bourbaki 1968, 7). No doubt he proposes an extremely literalized version of it, but this only amounts to exposing the *more geometrico*'s very essence. But this continuity is precisely what Lacan rejects, even if this rejection is only implicit in his affirmation that "letters constitute assemblages." By saying this, truth be told, he puts a fundamentally different figure in Bourbaki's place, one that we could call *hyper-Bourbakism.* Just as he had once added a hyper-structural hypothesis to structuralism.

Where pre-Bourbakist mathematics makes use of *rational* coherence, stemming from the Greeks, Bourbaki makes use of literal consistency alone. But he considers it to be homogenous to the former. Lacan, basing himself on a hyper-Bourbakism, tightens the noose even more: if there were any literal consistency, it could not but be imaginary, because consistency is always a variant of tethering; but there is not any literal consistency, because literality is not of the same nature as consistency.

The specific function of mathematics, as the matheme isolates it, can thus be summarized as follows: as Bourbaki articulates it and as Lacan, driven by hyper-Bourbakism, disarticulates it, it offers a treasure trove of material for a non-imaginary and non-qualitative theory of thinking.

Recall that the general problem of psychoanalysis is that there is a thinking that does not meet the imaginary and qualitative criteria of thought (coherence, the excluded middle, discursivity, negation, etc.; in short: Aristotle). This is the only condition on which the most ambitious version of the equation of subjects can be sustained: the identity between the subject of the *cogito* and the Freudian subject. Psychoanalysis must therefore construct a theory of thinking that includes, not as an unexpected extension but as a constitutive property, a thinking that is disjoined from imaginary organizations. In Freud, this theory is almost entirely negative; what is positive about it does not deserve to be called a theory; at best it is an energetic or biological model. In Lacan there is an ambition to create a *positive* theory that, beyond the imaginary of thought, touches on its real.

Mathematics and all the formal disciplines are called upon to bring this program to fruition.

But we know that their extension has varied. In the paradigm of the first classicism, it includes the major disciplines of extended Galileism. Linguistics, especially, is expected to expose the mechanisms of a non-reflexive thinking, one that is nonconscious and non-Aristotelian. Of course, the same expectations hold for Bourbakist mathematics, Russellian and post-Russellian logic, and Lévi-Straussian anthropology. This is not a surprise, since the fundamental homogeneity of their formalizations was made into a hypothesis by the Discourse of Rome.

In the second classicism, the homogeneity is broken. Only mathematics remains, and it remains only in its hyper-Bourbakist version. Such is the major axis of a non-imaginary theory of thinking. The matheme brings its decisive status into the full light of day.

It is true that none of this would have been possible without extended Galileism. Let's add that it would not have been possible without Bourbaki, since Bourbaki alone, in a consistent manner, pursued the goal of a mathematics separated from quantity. This was an assumption that was necessary in order for structuralisms, especially linguistic ones, to be considered mathematical, even though they involve neither measurement nor even logico-mathematical deduction. This is true, but it is also true that something changes between the Rome Discourse and "L'Étourdit."

First of all is the fact that Lacan had gradually separated the specific agency of letters from the generalized symbolic: at the same time, the still humanist symbolic of Rome[17] is reduced to its bare minimum: the letter S in RSI. Second, Lacan more and more explicitly thematized a mathematics of letters [*le littéralisme dans la mathématique*]: in Rome, mathematics was still associated with rational continuity, but now it is presented only as an inconsistent jumble of dispersed written formulas. Third, he radically limited the mathematizing move in modern science: science is understood to no longer do anything but grab what it can from the jumble of writings, taking from them only what allows, bit by bit, for the transliteration of some aspect of the universe: even if mathematized physics were unified (which it is not), the mathematics of its mathematization would not have to be, because mathematics itself isn't. Fourth is the fact that from then on, when it comes to science's letters, Lacan no longer accepts help from any other source but strict mathematics, that of the pure mathematicians. Reread, of course, following the rules of the hyper-Bourbakist fragmentation.

Not only does this include mathematical logic; mathematical logic gives us its purest type: with it, it becomes clear that Euclid amounts to nothing, and that the real driving force of so-called demonstrations is a calculus with letters (sometimes called a "deduction" or "proof," but this doesn't matter). This logic is called "mathematical" for good reason, not because it contains mathematics as one of its branches (logicism), not because it speaks of mathematics and legitimizes its procedures (metamathematics), but because it fully displays what henceforth defines mathematicity as such.[18] Moreover, there is no contradiction in saying that the science of the real is, in free variation, mathematics or logic: both expressions involve the same property, literality.

Quite far from it being the case, then, that Koyré's hostility to logic must be shared, it is no longer even appropriate to agree with the indif-

CHAPTER 4

ference toward it of Koyréism's more moderate adherents. Because of its mere possibility, mathematical logic becomes the shibboleth of science: not so much due to its methods and its specific results, but because it brings out mathematicity's authentic essence. In this way, one of the most serious instabilities that marked the first classicism is repaired (see chapter 4, p. 73).[19]

But this success comes at the cost of a change in discourse. In "L'Étourdit," mathematics is nothing more than letters, but the letters of science are nothing more than strict mathematics, that is, calculus. Linguistics, Lévi-Strauss, and all of structuralism no longer contain anything that holds up before the least mathematical writing. The matheme is the sign, the effect, and the name of this change. The matheme becomes at once both permissible and necessary, insofar as the mathematical field is no longer anything but a rendering into letters [*littéralisation*] and there is no longer any rendering of science into letters outside of the explicitly mathematical field.

Jakobson had been the harbinger of extra-mathematical mathematics, which we can easily relate to the symbolic. The session of Seminar XX dedicated to him is in fact a goodbye to this former figure. Not to Jakobson himself, who became, thanks to his subjective power, the bearer of other, new insights, but to Rome.[20] This is what the theme of "linguistrickery" signals, ("my linguistrickery," Lacan says); the [French] term [*linguisterie*] is formed in the same way that we describe the actions characteristic of artisans we disdain (*piracy, fraud, cheating, sham*) [*piraterie, escroquerie, tricherie, fumisterie*] and is based on the word *linguist* rather than on the word *linguistics*—linguistrickery is just not the same as language-trickery. Avowed linguists are no longer mathematicians, as they had once been; if they were overtly what they are in secret, they would reveal themselves to be gold diggers, errant and solitary navigators, pillagers of sea wrecks rather than scholars—subjects in exile.

The Rome Discourse dreams of a mathematics so consistent with itself that it could expand its empire without trembling. From set theory, correctly axiomatized, one could conclude that there was no gap from Freud to Jakobson or Levi-Strauss: a true royal road. *Encore* [i.e., *Seminar XX*] ends with the closing of the gate; Bourbaki's name, which contained all the sesames, is transformed into its opposite and the locks are set once and for all. The whole of the *Écrits* fits into the program of extended mathematics. But now we must hold that nothing that is mathematized therein directly conforms to the matheme. Neither the appendix of the "Seminar on 'The Purloined Letter,'" nor the formulas for metaphors and metonymy, nor the optical scheme in "Remarks on Daniel Lagache's Presentation," nor the graphs and writings of "Subversion of the Subject" are mathemes, even though they derive from a mathematization. This is not only because the concept of the matheme was not yet formally constructed, but because the concept of the matheme sets up a configuration that radically excludes what seemed to be announced in 1953 and remained in effect in 1966.

Strictly speaking, we could even hold that the matheme only exists with and after "L'Étourdit." In which case, even discourse theory does not entirely meet its conditions. To treat discourse theory in terms of the matheme, while not being entirely illegitimate, would be a retroactive forcing: furthermore, it would be a forcing performed on the letters of the first classicism, sometimes correcting them, sometimes confirming them (see, for example, *Seminar XX*, Lacan 1998 [1975], 28–29). Thus the second classicism can grasp the first and transform it by deriving mathemes from it. Nonetheless, in psychoanalysis there would be only one primary matheme: that of the sexual writings. This is consistent with Freud: psychoanalysis says only one thing, always the same, which is that there is sex. This also explains why Lacan prefers to speak of the matheme in the singular, rather than in the plural. In the second classicism, mathematization is needed more than ever: if it is assumed to be possible, it is so thanks to a mathematics withdrawn into its own fragmentation; if it is accomplished, it is purely thanks to a lucky strike in the game of letters.

4. The Visibility of the Literal

But something exists that is called the Borromean knot. It has a definitive property: it suffices for one of the three loops it knots together to fall away for all the others to disperse. But this is a property of the literal as such, and more precisely of the mathematical literal.

Barely a year after "L'Étourdit," which introduces the matheme, nine months after giving a hyper-Bourbakist reading of mathematics, the knot is called "the best basis we can provide for that by which mathematical language proceeds." Why? Because "the nature of mathematical language, once it is sufficiently isolated in terms of its requirements of pure demonstration, is such that everything that is put forward there—not so much in the spoken commentary as in the very handling of letters—assumes that if one of the letters doesn't stand up, all the others . . . disperse" (*Seminar XX*, Lacan 1998 [1975], 128). Three propositions are advanced here: first, the mathematics that the matheme is based on is a mathematics separated from deduction, which is taken both to be established and of no significance: this is what the interpolated clause

"once it is sufficiently isolated in terms of its requirements of pure demonstration" means; this is the very heart of the second classicism. Second,
mathematics, separated from deduction, consists of the pure literal: the
manipulation of letters, and not spoken commentary, which is always part
of a line of reasoning. Third, Borromeanism is the support of this mathematics, since Borromeanism is nothing more nor less than the fact that
it suffices for one loop to fall away for the others to be dispersed; but this
property is deemed to be the best and perhaps the only analogue of the
property that defines the literal as such.

However, and this is not any less surprising, the knot, insofar as it is
Borromean, turns out to be appropriate for structuring, or more exactly
for mathematizing, an element of the doctrine which had been present
since the first classicism. Namely, the troika of the real, the symbolic, and
the imaginary. In certain respects, we could say that this troika sums up
the hard kernel of the Rome Discourse: in any case, it is what remains
after the disruption that is inflicted on the first classicism. Up to then,
the doctrine was increasingly able to articulate how it understands the
real, the symbolic, and the imaginary; however, it could not say anything
robust about how they coexisted. Henceforth, by the kind of happy accident that we sometimes find in letters, the Borromean knot turns out
to offer the most clear and most fertile solution.

Previously the capital letters R, S, I could be taken as simple ab-
breviations, without any other rule for how they should be used but descriptive convenience, and without any other legitimacy but the fact that
they are initials. When each one of them becomes the label for a loop
that is knotted in a Borromean fashion to two others, they turn out to
be caught up in a real law that constrains them. They allow for a calculus with classical experiential categories (inhibition, symptom, anxiety,
jouissance; see Lacan 1975a; Lacan 1975b, 95–105). They then become well
and truly letters. What the second classicism still contained of the first,
constituting a substrate common to both, can be inscribed in the Borromean arrangement in the form of three letters: from then on the whole
doctrine can be stated on the basis of a single, infinitely rich, matrix.

This is a matrix that goes so far as to provide an ultimate and complete elucidation of the equation of subjects. Through the course of the
years, all three of the affirmations it contains had been given a precise
status. All except the first: Lacan had repeated throughout his oeuvre that
psychoanalysis operates on a subject. Once this is admitted, everything
else quickly gets established: that this subject is the Cartesian subject, that
it is determined by science, and that it is represented by a signifier for
another signifier. The affirmation itself remains. But what does it mean,
exactly?

Just after having introduced the knot, and thanks to it, Lacan strips away its veils. This affirmation is a hypothesis, *Lacan's hypothesis*: "the unconscious, I do not enter there, no more than did Newton, without a hypothesis. My hypothesis is that the individual who is affected by the unconscious is the same individual who constitutes what I call the subject of a signifier" (*Seminar XX*, Lacan 1998 [1975], 142).[21]

After this, everything falls into place. The equation of subjects identified the subject of science with the subject that psychoanalysis operates on: they were one and the same, because they were one and the same with the subject of signifiers. With Lacan's hypothesis we see that the expression "the subject that psychoanalysis operates on" is to be doubled: there is the individual affected by an unconscious, which is what analytic practice in its most technical sense deals with; and there is the subject defined by the theory of unspecified structure: this is the subject of a signifier. These are not two subjects who make up one, but one subject and one individual who, radically distinct from the subject, coincides with it. This means that the distinction is irreducible, and that being the same means being Other.

We can see the doctrine:

Premise one: *The subject of science is the subject of a signifier* (hypothesis of the subject of signifiers, formulated by the first classicism, preserved in the second).

Premise two: *The subject of a signifier coincides with an individual affected by an unconscious* (Lacan's hypothesis, formulated only in the second classicism).

Premise three: *The practice of psychoanalysis operates on an individual affected by an unconscious* (Freud's foundational hypothesis).

Conclusion: *By a coincidence, psychoanalysis encounters a subject in its practice.*[22]

I've called this a clarification. What we are dealing with here is in fact more like a cancellation, to be thought of as an *Aufhebung*. The equation of subjects, with which everything started, comes undone at the very moment it acquires its full status. Not that its pivotal point isn't preserved; instead, what was stated as an equation is now stated in terms of a coincidence and an encounter. And if someone were to ask what coincidence and encounter are, the knot would offer clarity: it is a matter of a real determination (the subject), an imaginary determination (the individual), and a symbolic determination (the signifier) knotted together in a Borromean way. If someone were to ask what a subject is, the definition of the signifier would suffice; it would suffice, which means that nothing more would be necessary, especially not the metaphysical subject. The axiom of the subject (chapter 2, p. 17) no longer has any status or utility, since the subject is immediately included in the signifier as such.

Let's be careful: this is not an overturning. The axiom and the equation distinguished the individual from the subject. Knot theory makes it possible for the individual and the subject to be superimposed. But in Borromean logic, they can only be superimposed because they are absolutely heterogeneous. Lacan's hypothesis, by speaking in terms of an encounter, restates what the axiom of the subject posits as a distinction; at the same time it renders this axiom superfluous.

The metaphysical subject's irrelevance corresponds to the axiom of the subject's decline. Hence, references to thought lose their urgency: "the unconscious is not the fact that being thinks" (*Seminar XX*, Lacan 1998 [1975], 104); in fact, "'man thinks with his soul' means that man thinks with Aristotle's thought" (ibid., 111) In other words, there is no thought but one that is imaginarized and has qualities (resemblances, negation, the law of the excluded middle, *dictum de omni et nullo*, categories, judgment, doubt, etc.), with which the unconscious has nothing to do. This should be connected to the proposition "the signifier is stupid" (ibid., 20), from which we could derive the proposition "the signifier does not think"; in other words, it is no longer the case that signifiers articulate a thought without qualities. Because in fact this thought does not exist: there is no thought but the thought of Aristotle.

Reciprocally, what science requires, that which is "without qualities," is no longer called *thought*. This is how we have to understand the fact that Lacan, returning to Freud, but also to Marx, henceforth prefers to speak of *work*: the unconscious is "knowledge that does not think, or calculate, or judge—which doesn't prevent it from being at work" (*Television*, Lacan 1990a [1973], 14). Once again, the definition of the unconscious as "it thinks" is not really overturned here; it is just violently displaced. In order for the unconscious to be an "it thinks," we know that it is necessary that there be a thought without qualities; psychoanalysis has entirely succeeded in establishing its existence, yet at the very moment it succeeds it turns out that thought no longer needs to be spoken of at all.

If only the thought of Aristotle exists, then that which is without qualities must be given a different name. Marx is at his most helpful here. The work in question—the work of the unconscious, of signifiers—is the undifferentiated and nondescript work whose theory is produced in volume 1 of *Capital*. This is a work without qualities. Thus the subject supposed to underlie unconscious knowledge—the subject without qualities—can be called "the ideal worker" (*Television*, Lacan 1990a [1973], 14; ". . . ou pire," Lacan 2001g [1975], 551, which reminds us of *The Worker*, perhaps an innocent flirtation with Jünger?).[23]

If the signifier is essentially separated from thought and if thought is henceforth inseparable from qualities, the subject without qualities is strictly the subject of the signifier and not the subject of thought; it cancels itself out into an imaginary individual the very moment that it thinks anything at all, especially "I am." Hence the *cogito*, contrary to what the first classicism advanced, is not the emergence of the subject but its submersion. The *logion* "it thinks where I am not" is replaced by the *logion* or *quasi-logion* "where it speaks, it enjoys, and it knows nothing" (used as an exergue for session 9, *Seminar XX*, Lacan 1998 [1975], 104). The *it speaks* [*ça parle*] and *lalangue* (in one word), which is just the substantive form of *it speaks*, absorb the *it thinks* [*ça pense*]. Descartes becomes useless and uncertain.[24]

The homonymy that connected the axiom of the subject to metaphysics no longer brings about any knowledge-effect; as for the development of any eventual synonyms, access to them is henceforth barred. Lacan puts radical Cartesians and any transcendental ambitions on notice. The *Cahiers pour l'Analyse* project is met with a flat refusal.

Thanks to the knot, the second classicism thus seems to incorporate, arrange, and redefine the heritage of the first. The knot takes up what is essential about mathematics for psychoanalysis: its literality. At the same time, all the difficulties connected to science's Core Doctrine are taken to be resolved: psychoanalysis is in principle mathematized and it knows how to spell out what mathematization means. The uselessness of extended Galileisms is confirmed. The theory of unspecified structure is taken up, but it is henceforth just the regional theory of the S loop.[25] The equation of subjects, in which science's Core Doctrine and the theory of unspecified structure are joined together, is finally clarified, and undone.

We see here the sort of ideal movement that is celebrated in the history of the sciences. The instabilities that affect a first model lead to the emergence of a second model which, sometimes, after a long while, resolves them. Considered this way, the Borromean knot gives force and confirmation to the matheme. Its definition makes the royal road to psychoanalysis as wide open as possible, insofar as it relates to modern science.[26]

5. Antiphilosophy

Psychoanalysis has established that it is the discourse of the subject. But it no longer needs philosophy to make it clear what a subject is. If philosophy is useless to it, then it is noxious and must be designated as such. The moment has come for "antiphilosophy."

This word came as a surprise. References to philosophers seemed to be inseparable from Lacan's oeuvre. Freud remained reserved about them—more Austrian than German in this respect—and was always more inclined to use art and literature as supports rather than philosophy. Lacan constantly cited the *corpus philosophorum*. By speaking of antiphilosophy, did he decide to contradict himself?

The theme does have a specific date. It occurs with the reorganization of the Department of Psychoanalysis at the University Paris-VIII in 1975. It reappeared in 1980 on the occasion of a polemic started by Louis Althusser. Here as elsewhere, however, it would be vain to confine ourselves to anecdotes. That the reorganization of the Department of Psychoanalysis had to go through curious, unpleasant, and interminable negotiations with the Department of Philosophy, such that it led to a veritable conflict of the faculties . . . this is not without importance, as much as it might make us smile today. But none of this was enough to justify the creation of such a violent word. It can only be fully explained by causes that are equal to its violence. Were it only for chronological reasons, the causes are manifestly to be found in the general arrangement of the second classicism, that is to say, in the matheme.

We know that for a long time Lacan was hesitant about including himself in the university's organization, and was content with the support that it was able to provide him on the margins. After 1970 he came to terms with the idea, and perhaps wished, that a department would rally around him. A change that had multiple causes. We cannot underestimate the overturning that happened to the institution of the French university in 1968. The question is to know how Lacan interpreted it. There are several reasons to think that he took the university to be a decadent apparatus; precisely for this reason, he concluded that it would be no big deal to use the means that were still available to him within such an obsolescent institution (just as Christians did not hesitate to use the Empire, once they were assured that its crisis was incurable. Even if it meant presenting themselves as its best guarantor).

But this does not go far enough: the institution of the university is based on an act of transmission; the legitimacy of a department of psychoanalysis at a university can then only be supported by a secure doctrine on the transmissibility of psychoanalysis. If a department at a university were in fact able to be accepted as a venue appropriate for the teaching of Lacan (a new decision, let's recall), it was because the doctrine of the matheme was complete. Taking the university route is not only contemporary with the second classicism; the latter is required as one of the former's necessary conditions (which does not mean to say that it is a necessary consequence; on this point, experts disagree).

Now, the reorganization of the department is summarized under the heading of antiphilosophy. Thus it is the matheme alone that justifies this word. More precisely, antiphilosophy is just another name for the matheme.

The thesis is thus:

Philosophy and the matheme of psychoanalysis are mutually exclusive.

This argument is in fact easy to construct. It suffices that we take literally what so many philosophers (not all of them) say themselves: that they rely on Greek philosophy, without any major break. But Greek philosophy is profoundly linked to the world of *epistèmè*. In certain respects, it founds this world. *Epistèmè*, with its structure in which *theoria* is distinguished from *praxis*, is only completely legitimated by philosophy. In return, the philosopher is never able to be indifferent to the possibility that there is *epistèmè* (whether he denies or affirms this possibility): namely, a knowledge that requires the soul, and summons it forth.

The word *philosophy* itself touches on the foundations of such a world. The necessary and its pomp, resemblance and its duties, the soul and its purifications . . . this is what philosophy and *epistèmè* develop together; perhaps the best name for them is *sophia*, a wisdom that one must love as oneself (*philein*). Modern science renounces all this. Psychoanalysis explicitly develops this renunciation. It is thus, strictly speaking, the inverse of philosophy.

The conclusion is thus:

There is no philosophy that is wholly in sync with modern science, even if it is contemporary with it.

This does in fact give it some value. The contemporary philosophy of modern science contains arrangements that are foreign to it. Whence its link to the essence of mathematics, as long as this is not defined in linguistic terms. Even when it does not deny the major break, philosophy keeps it open and problematic; it requires us to think about it. Some would say that philosophy is in the position of an absolute reference point.

But psychoanalysis, for its part, is intrinsically in sync with modern science; compared to philosophy it thus belongs to another (logical or chronological) time. Still, it is necessary for it to be able to express its synchrony. After Freud, it only had at its disposal the corrupted terms of the ideal science. This is why, in the first classicism's configuration, psychoanalysis used philosophy. It was a matter of putting some distance between itself and the ideal science such as Freud and the good little Freudians had imagined the latter. The axiom of the subject and its homonymy are the chief witnesses to this.

Freud had put his trust in humanist culture—literature, history, archaeology. Having recourse to them was not sufficient; one could have predicted that it would be even less sufficient after the institutional, military, political, and moral collapse of the lands in which classical humanism had long survived—the Germany of Melanchthon, the Austria of the Jesuits, the France of the Dreyfusard Sorbonne. Especially since the ideal science had gained in power; after 1945 it was on the side of the winners. The victory of the liberal democracy of engineers and merchants was also the victory of the most obtuse of sciences.[27]

The return to Freud thus meant taking a detour through regions that Freud had kept himself away from. Against the distorted scientism of the International Psychoanalytic Association, the arms of philosophy were at that point stronger than the arms of culture. To get across how closely he belonged to the universe of science, Lacan first of all had to get rid of English-language psychoanalysis's false and strictly imitative inclusion in science, far from its native lands. Only philosophy could serve this end, since it alone presented itself, in terms of systematicity and demonstration, as Other to science.

The repeated use that Lacan made of philosophy during this time does not at all contradict the fact that it is in a relationship of mutual exclusion to psychoanalysis. Quite to the contrary, it assumes this exclusion. This exclusion is what allows philosophy to be committed to lifting away the imposing mass of the ideal science and its institutional counterfeits. Using philosophy is the exact reverse of antiphilosophy. This also means that the latter is the obverse of the former.

The fact remains that a reversal happened, with the creation of a word. We have passed from the obverse to the reverse, from heads to tails. The fact is that Lacan no doubt thought that his first battle, against the ideal science, had been won. The ideal science of the WASPs, at least. Perhaps thanks to 1968, which was supposed to have put a stop to its effortless expansion. Perhaps thanks as well to the lunar module, in which the irruption of a real brought about by science rids science of its imaginary ballast, establishing its pure mathematization ("scientific discourse was able to bring about the moon landing, where thought becomes witness to a performance of the real, and with mathematics using no other apparatus than a form of language," *Television*, Lacan 1990a [1973], 36).

To these external causes, which have the value of a symptom, an internal one is added: the appearance of the theory of the matheme, strengthened by the display of the knot. At the time of the second classicism, the term "antiphilosophy" is specifically about transmission. At the time of the first classicism it did not need to be uttered, because the problem of the complete transmissibility of psychoanalysis had not been highlighted. It is true that during this period Lacan emphasizes the importance of psychoanalysis's relation to modern science; it is true that he incessantly uses mathematical objects, but he does not say that the only possible transmission happens with the mathematical letter. Because in fact he had not completely made the doctrine of the letter autonomous, and because he had not defined mathematics by letters. As soon as these determining theses are put forward, regarding letters, mathematics and transmission, the reversal can be accomplished.

Moreover, all we have to do is quote: "In order for it to be the language that is most propitious to scientific discourse, mathematics is the science without conscience that our good old Rabelais promised, *one with respect to which a philosophy can only remain blocked up*" ("L'Étourdit," Lacan 2001f, 452; my emphasis); "the advent of the real, that is, the moon landing . . . *without the philosopher (for the newspaper makes every man a philosopher) caring about it*" (*Television*, Lacan 1990a [1973], 36–37; my emphasis); "*I rise up*, if I may say, against philosophy. What is certain is that it is a thing of the finite. Even if I expect that a discharge will emerge from it" ("Monsieur A.," Lacan 1980, 17; Lacan's emphasis).[28]

We should not be surprised, then, that after having incessantly frequented philosophical texts, after having educated himself in the concept by reading Hegel, after having translated Heidegger, commented on Plato and Descartes, and cited Aristotle and St. Thomas Aquinas, Lacan invents a word that philosophers, it must be said, have collectively taken as an insult.

In this respect, philosophy is like politics. Their co-belonging becomes a theorem: "Metaphysics has never been anything else, and will not continue to be anything else, except that which busies itself with blocking up the hole of politics. That is its inspiration," Lacan writes in 1973, addressing himself especially to Heidegger ("Introduction à l'édition allemande," Lacan 2001h, 555). Because politics, too, turns out to be radically out of sync with the modern universe.

Is it an accident if, when it speaks of the State, of democracy, of domination, of freedom, politics speaks in Greek and Latin (of course, when it does speak at all; usually it mumbles)? This fundamental dissynchrony results in a principled indifference on the part of psychoanalysis. Because the two do not belong either to the same world or the same universe.

Just as science and politics have nothing to do with each other—except committing crimes—because they do not belong to the same world or the same universe, similarly psychoanalysis has nothing to do with politics—except the uttering of stupidities. Such was, recall, Freud's position: "political agnosticism," "indifference" ("Science and Truth," Lacan 2006m, 728–29).[29] An antipolitics, one could say, running parallel to antiphilosophy.

Indifference, taken in this sense, does not necessarily lead to keeping quiet about the objects spoken of in politics. Lacan did not remain systematically mute in this respect. Let's agree to set aside the very general remarks he makes about the course of the world—they are scattered among the protreptic interventions that Lacan often did not bother to take up again, and are limited, for the most part, to broad generalizations: compared to most opinions they are flashes of insight, but they fall short when it comes to knowledge. There is also something else to take into account; namely, the theory of the four discourses. This amounts to an intervention into the empirical field of the objects that politics—as practice and as thought—busies itself with. Whether it is successful or not is not the question. What it is important to emphasize is the overall intention. It is obvious that it does nothing to change the radical indifference that Freud considered the only possible choice, since the most diverse political propositions can be made to appear in it as different values of one and the same variable.

There is likewise a radical philosophical indifference in psychoanalysis.

This is in fact the reason for the overabundant references to the *corpus philosophorum*. One must be profoundly indifferent about philosophy to use so many technical concepts and to make explicit (or not) allusions so freely; or, what amounts to the same thing, one must hold that philosophy is a constellation of brilliant texts but does not constitute a thought. We find antiphilosophy here again, in the form of the most expansive philosophical erudition.

Just as political indifference does not stop anyone from occasionally speaking about politics (indifference in politics is not indifference to politics), antiphilosophy should not stop anyone from speaking about what philosophy speaks of: indifference in philosophy is not indifference to philosophy. In fact, we should go further: psychoanalysis not only has the right but the duty to speak about what philosophy speaks about, since it deals with exactly the same objects. In *Television*, Lacan agrees to answer the question he is asked under the triple heading "knowledge, hope, acting," and he does not object to this question inherited from Kant by arguing that it has lost its relevance. We could certainly see this as a merely erudite encounter. However, the relation is more intrinsic.

The point at which psychoanalysis intervenes can in fact be summarized this way: it is in the movement from the prior instant when the speaking being could have been infinitely other than it is—in body and in thought—to the following instant when the speaking being, by virtue of its very contingency, has become the equivalent of an eternal necessity. Because ultimately psychoanalysis speaks of only one thing: the conversion of each subjective singularity into a law as necessary as the laws of nature, as contingent as they are, and also as absolute.

Now, this is a moment that philosophy has always dealt with. In a sense, we could say that it even invented it. But, in order to describe it, philosophy generally went outside of the universe. But psychoanalysis is nothing if it does not maintain, as the linchpin of its doctrine, that there is nothing outside of the universe. In this and this alone lies what is structural and non-chronological about its relation to modern science.

At the same time, we see that philosophy and psychoanalysis speak of exactly the same thing, in terms that are all the more identical the more they aim at an opposite effect. Thus, the word "antiphilosophy" can be interpreted more completely; it is constructed in the same way as the name of the Antichrist is—as St. John presented it before Nietzsche did. "They went out from us, but they were not of us; for if they had been of us, they would no doubt have continued with us" (1 John 2:19). Philosophers could thus speak this way about Lacanians; more pertinently, they could recall that the Antichrist, as such, would speak exactly like Christ. His discourse requires the discourse it doesn't want to have anything to do with; it resembles it absolutely, it says the same things, using the same terms, precisely because it has no relation to it.

The only difference with St. John is that moderns, not believing in finitude, do not believe in the Last Judgment. If the Antichrist and Christ seek each other's disappearance, it is because the time is near: "there are now several antichrists: by this we know that it is the final hour," the Apostle writes (1 John 2:18). For antiphilosophy and philosophy, however, time is infinitely open. In this infinity, their mutual exclusion becomes a mutual envelopment; the point of each one will have its inverted correlate in the other; each will take turns being the dead god and the purple shroud.

5

The Deconstruction

The matheme, however, will meet with its own consummation. Subsequent events confirm this. The doctrine of the matheme was linked to an institution: the École Freudienne; this school was called a school, and Freudian, because it was based on the threefold hypothesis that something about Freud can be completely transmitted, that the place where complete transmission happens is a school, and that the means of complete transmission is, in such a place, the matheme. The school acted on the outside world with its review entitled *Scilicet* (whose motto was "you may know what the École Freudienne thinks of it"; to make it complete, we'll add "thanks to the matheme"); this review was modeled on Bourbaki, because mathematics is the model for literal transmission and because Bourbaki is the model for literal mathematics. But the school was dissolved for an instant. Even if another school did replace it at the very next moment, we cannot pretend the dissolution did not take place.[1] The review *Scilicet* disappeared. The names and forms (with their signed articles) of the reviews that succeeded it followed other, more classical, rules. In a similar way, Bourbakism was at that point finished in mathematics, to an extent that Lacan could not ignore.

It is unthinkable that historical accidents would suffice to explain the connections among so many discontinuities. Especially since Lacan's institutional will was always the symptom of a core doctrinal event. A certain French tradition expects thinkers to be satisfied with what exists, for better or for worse, instead of transforming the arrangement of things; Lacan did not adhere to this tradition. In this respect he was close to Mallarmé. Mallarmé believed that it was permissible for a subject to create institutions; he believed it as long as he believed in the Book. It is true that he left behind hardly any followers. We know quite well that the Book did not become part of Society; Mallarmé himself perhaps ended up having his own doubts about it. Valéry, at any rate, the most affectionate of his disciples, hastened to add that when it came to institutions, for poets there was no alternative to conformism.

As for the Seminar, it did not conform. It was an institutional creation, no less robust than the École Freudienne, and perhaps more audacious. We find Mallarmé here again at each step (the cartels of the École owed something to the arithmetic of the Book). I am referring to Mallarmé but, quite obviously, Freud must also be mentioned: that a man who rallied around the ideal of science thought it was possible to create, outside of academies, outside of government authorities, outside of churches, outside of professional unions, something like a new profession and something like the International Psychoanalytic Association, is, when one thinks about it, properly outrageous; the first thing that a modern scholar learns is that when it comes to careers and scientific institutions, creation is difficult and rarely succeeds. They rarely outlast the biological or legal death of their founders.

Lacan's institutional will, like Mallarmé's and Freud's, is an exception. To his own way of thinking it was only legitimate, however, when it was backed up by a doctrine. It is certainly permissible for a subject to create institutions dealing with knowledge—on just one condition: that this subject can, without scandal or ridicule, be taken as a subject supposed to know. It is thus appropriate to grant the greatest importance to institutional upheavals. These are not just about palace intrigue, but involve Lacanian knowledge itself.

The École Freudienne found support for its core doctrine in the doctrine of the matheme—which explained the sense in which it was permissible to know, and thus the sense in which a school was a sufficient (or necessary) way to act on this permission. So the fact that the school was dissolved for an instant can mean only one thing: that the matheme too had been dissolved. And just as the school that was rebuilt after the dissolution was not the same as what preceded it, likewise the matheme that was reaffirmed was not the same.

Texts do not contradict the conclusion that we are led to by the sequence of events. It is clear that the use of mathematics changes with Seminar XX. Basically, references to mathematics from then on get replaced by the theory of the Borromean knot. Not without reason. The knot brings us within reach of letters, especially of mathematical letters. To shed light on the laws of Borromeanism is thus to shed light on the foundations of the matheme as such; it is to bring to light the principle of its efficacy. So it is right that the whole effort bears on what is supposed to be the determining point; if speaking about nothing else but the knot amounts to speaking about the only necessary thing, then it is necessary to limit oneself to that.

But one thing should strike us from the get-go: even though there is a way to approach the knots through mathematization, this is not what Lacan emphasizes about them. More precisely still, it seems as if Lacan is only interested in the knot because of how resistant it is to any integral mathematization: "there is no theory of knots. Currently, there is no mathematical formalization applicable to knots" (*Seminar XX*, Lacan 1998 [1975], 129).

The knot thus turns out to be something completely different from the numerous topological objects—the Möbius strip, the cross-cap—that were used before. There is a mathematical theory of these; even if it is not taken up directly by Lacan, its general possibility means that the realm of mathematics, offering a general theory of any matheme, does not need to be left behind ("[my topological exposé] was able to be made from an algebra consisting purely of letters" ("L'Étourdit," Lacan 2001f [1972], 472). For the knot, the braids, etc., the question is entirely different. No doubt they come from mathematics, but rather as curiosities; the knot exhausts itself in its tirelessly varied displays ("little constructions," *Seminar XX*, Lacan 1998 [1975], 129) and does not need to be integrally written in order for its efficacy to be legitimate. Of course, this did not prevent mathematicians from trying to mathematize the knot. Some made brilliant attempts at it, under Lacan's attentive gaze. Perhaps, at the moment I am writing this, it has been established that they or others have completely succeeded. It still remains the case that the knot did not have to await their efforts in order for it to be able to play a role in discourse.

There are certainly precursors to this. Recall the paradox at the beginning of the Core Doctrine of science; after Galileo and Descartes, three things had to be held simultaneously: that the universe is entirely susceptible to a mathematized science, that it is infinite, and that the infinite is not a mathematically clear object—at least it wasn't when Galilean science was constructed.[2] It was nonetheless the case that rather quickly the infinite yielded to a calculus and to mathematical writings, as opaque as their meaning was up to at least Bolzano. Such that one could recognize in its emergence the victory of the literal as such, rather than its defeat.

The knot is something entirely different; it is antinomical to letters and, because of this, antinomical to the matheme.[3] Because a major split is opened up: the knot can be assigned letters (for example, R, S, I), its Borromeanism shows what the literal is, but it is not itself completely rendered into letters [*littéralisé*]: "there is no mathematical formalization applicable to knots." This means that a nonliteral object is given the task of revealing what the essence of the literal is. In letters themselves there is nothing to be found that lets it be sufficiently rendered into letters.

Of course, this reminds us of the many ways in which radical incompletion is a recurring theme for Lacan; without being abandoned, it apparently lost its dramatic intensity, at least as long one stuck to a mathematization that conformed to Lacanian wishes: scattered, not deductive, local. But with the knot all the drama returns: we can rediscover some of his former *logia* in them if we modify them slightly; there is no Other of the Other, no metalanguage; there is no matheme of the matheme, no letter of the letter; there is only the knot, which continues to resist complete literalization, however far its literalization is pushed.

At the time of *Encore*, this resistance was not thought to be eternally irreducible. Nothing prevented us from thinking that mathematics would one day be able to include what is specific to Borromeanism. But as the mathematical work advanced, over the course of the later seminars, we see not only that success was elusive, but that if it were to be attained, at that very moment everything that made it special would be lost. Not only is the knot not mathematized, but it only functions by not being so.

At least, this is the case if mathematics as such remained what it seemed to be. But that was no longer true either. Bourbaki, reinterpreted in an appropriate way, contained the foundations for the doctrine of the letter, insofar as it was distinct from the doctrine of the signifier. But the rumor was spreading, and it would quickly become too powerful to ignore: what if Bourbaki were dead?[4]

This would mean that there was a future for mathematics in which literality would perhaps have a subalternate status. By way of Bourbaki, this would also affect hyper-Bourbakism. Lacan perhaps suspected this by the end of Seminar XX. Let's assume he did; the knot, as the support of the *mathematical* letter, would no longer be the support of anything essential since, by hypothesis, letters are no longer essential to mathematics. It would find itself brought back to its own absence of literality. The field of letters would offer nothing more than an occasion for mourning: a mourning for the mathematical letter and its power. Not that the knot has nothing to say about letters, not that there are no letters, not that there is no mathematics, but the knot only says something about letters because it excludes itself from them; letters find themselves in the realm of their own failure; mathematics, if it still has any force, is not of the literal. Reading the seminars that follow *Seminar XX*, we cannot avoid the conviction that everything happened exactly this way.

Just as a gnarled stick is transformed into a serpent before Pharaoh's eyes, the knot, once a support for the imagination, is transformed into a destructive animal. The destroyer of letters. It is not the case that Lacan renounces letters, but if there were to be a letter, he had to search for it elsewhere from that point forward. New places take over from mathematics and the curiosities that it offered; the roads led to Joyce, the poem . . . *Literature*, in a word. This movement no doubt begins in *Encore*. But in that exhilarating text, the matheme is at its peak and the poem makes an appearance only in order to confirm it. Saussure and Jakobson, abandoned as guarantors of the first classicism, come back in a new position, that of linguist-subjects (recall that this is the upshot of linguistrickery), capable, as subjects, and as linguists, of assuring a transitivity between mathematical and poem-atical letters. Thus we find in *Encore* an equivalence, at the level of letters, between the two arrangements of the matheme and the *poème*, in Parmenides: "Fortunately, Parmenides actually wrote poems. Doesn't he use linguistic devices—the linguist's testimony takes precedence here—that closely resemble mathematical articulation, alternation after succession, framing after alternation?" (*Seminar XX*, Lacan 1998 [1975], 22). Notice the adverb: fortune makes it the case that letters that come from Literature and letters that come from Numbers are in harmony with each other. The master of symmetries, Jakobson, who came in person in order to speak to the seminar, testifies to it even more. As he did earlier, but for new reasons: "one changes discourse," Lacan repeats in his presence, "a new love" he adds, citing Rimbaud (ibid., 16).

After *Encore*, however, the symmetry is broken. The poem is certainly reassuring; could it not, some day, assuming the knot gives out, offer a more robust support for literality? But the poem is also troubling; because it proliferates. If it is what the linguist says it is ("alternation after succession, framing after alternation"), it emerges at every twinkling that the (aleatory or not) interplay of any facet paired to any other produces on the crystal of language. The homonymical puns that are developed in Lacan's remarks starting from the 1970s are not witticisms; they are detached from any *Witz*; one by one they form a literal cellule, an atom of poematic calculus, foreclosed from any subject.[5] At first able to be thought of as completely homomorphic to mathematical letters (it is in this sense that, in "L'Étourdit," when the matheme is introduced, the homophonic play is already present, starting with the title itself), they are like mathemes produced by *lalangue* itself, answering to the mathemes constructed by discourse. Strictly analogous to the Big Dipper, inscribing by a stroke of luck the number Seven in the starry sky, exactly the same number that can be used to make a calculus, they sparkle, in the galaxy of *lalangue*, like constellations—at once contingent and architectonic.[6]

But it so happens that mathematics is no longer unquestionably literal. The analogy is ruined. At this point the homophonies become the only remaining trace of literality, no longer symmetrical, but now placeholders for a worn-out matheme. Their proliferation offsets the silent showing of the knots. But, also, it confirms and repeats it.

Because these two games devour each other. To the point that each devours itself. The poem, polymerized to the unlimited infinity of *lalangue*, explodes fixedly into the abyss.[7] On the one hand there are the quiet knots, and on the other, simultaneously disconnected from itself and omnipresent, is the poem, attested to and abolished by its own over-abundance. Each of the homophonic games, in the titles of the seminars, in the written elaborations, in the incessant return to Joyce, is like a pod containing within itself the possibility of a letter coming from language alone, entirely different from what mathematics, now deficient, proposed—and yet given identical functions. Unless their opacity continually risks carrying the day. Constellations can always go cold from forgetfulness.[8]

At the same time, the hand closes itself, finger by finger, over the materiality of bits of string. As another hand, once before, did with truths.

Until the last act of a teaching tirelessly pursued over so many years, the last word of so many amazing concepts, dazzling analyses, audacious writings, perpetual inventions, becomes a silent manipulation, indistinguishable in the eyes of the vulgar from a solitary mania.

It would certainly be different from one if it assured the complete transmission of the literal. But this would spring the trap. If it succeeded, the knot would prove, by its real, that there is at least one case in which complete transmission does not go through the matheme—since the knot, not being a letter, is not a matheme. If it failed, however, nothing would be transmitted of what makes it the case that letters transmit. Only the crystal of language would remain, materialized in the protean poem, indefinitely multiplied in puns; but then would transmission be complete? Would it have ever even begun?

At the end of the journey the knot purloined the letters, even if letters ended up arriving at their destination because of this very diversion. It became an anti-mathematics. After the antilinguistics in the doctrine of the signifier, made explicit in the doctrine of homophony, after the antipolitics induced by the theory of discourses, after the antiphilosophy contained in the first classicism and made explicit in the second. In short, the discursive anachoresis was completed.

So the knot was mortal.

Seminar XX, which introduces it, holds an exceptional place in Lacan's oeuvre. Because of its doctrinal significance: the second Lacanian classicism is brought to completion in it, regarding both what makes it distinct from the first, and what it contains that is still attached to the first (hence the title of the seminar: *Encore*). By its form: the disjunction between the esoteric and the exoteric shows itself to be provisional; the oeuvre form joins together with the efficacy of protreptics. Finally, by its reversal, the stuff of tragedy: in its very perfection we find the seeds of what will kill it, of what will lead to *The Seminar* as such coming undone, from the first volume up to the last.

Admittedly, this is a strong conclusion. It should not be advanced carelessly. Those who witnessed the last seminars should, however, be close to taking this step. To think of the Lacan of this time irresistibly calls to mind Wittgenstein at the end of the *Tractatus*: one must remain silent about what does not let itself be said; that about which one must remain silent must be shown. Well, Lacan stayed silent, and Lacan showed.[9]

What was shown in silence is something without which the transmission of psychoanalysis would not be able to be completely accomplished. How can we avoid inductive reasoning here? If the matheme is abolished, then one can no longer say, one can only show; well, after Seminar XX, Lacan progressively ends up doing nothing but showing, and this is because the matheme had been abolished. At the same time, Galileism in psychoanalysis was abolished: "the analytic thing will not be mathematical. This is why the discourse of analysis differs from scientific discourse" (*Seminar XX*, Lacan 1998 [1975], 117).

It is no accident that Lacan will rediscover anti-Galilean formulas like "Nature abhors knots" (Lacan 1975c, 101). Apart from its form, emblematic of what any basic history of science attributes to Galileo's Aristotelian adversaries, such a *logion* entails a radical consequence: if nature abhors the knot and if the knot were to be a mathematical letter, then Nature and any mathematical letter would be incompatible, which is directly opposed to the foundational axiom of modern science. Either mathematized science has to be considered abolished, in which case the totality of the Core Doctrine falls, and along with it the second Lacanian classicism, insofar as it shares something in common with the first; or else the knot is not a letter, and it is thus not a matheme, in which case the second classicism is also abolished, insofar as it is distinct from the first. As is the case with the alienating *or*, one loses either way.

Thus, the second classicism was over at the very moment it seemed to be accomplished. Lacan himself put an end to it. Seminar XX, which is its peak, triggers its deconstruction. Everything was already smashed to pieces when Lacan chose, as 1980 approached, to be silent. On the one hand, the knot, on the other, the poem; bits of string and letters; silence and the pun. One thinks of Ethiopia.[10]

This is not so far from Wittgenstein. This is not the place to engage in a systematic study of their relationship. There is no doubt that Lacan read Wittgenstein; nor is there any doubt that he drew hardly any explicit conclusions from him. Besides, we can predict that some people will be in a hurry to read the two together; the circumstances are perfect for this: some new wings will thus be added to the Castle of Mist.

I will stick to the basics here. We'll state what we will call the *Wittgenstein problem*. Let's assume, as it seems we must, that according to Wittgenstein there is an antinomy between saying and showing. There is what is said and there is what is not said; the border between the two is real and impassable. What is not said is shown and one must remain silent about it; what is shown is shown in tableaux. Included among what is not said, and thus what is shown by tableaux, is the truth of what is said.

It is clear that Lacan, almost throughout his entire written oeuvre, held that the Wittgenstein problem was both real and manageable. That it did not lead to silence as a duty. In fact, Lacan had very early on encountered silence and its relation to truth—and he distanced himself from it. We have already brought up (chapter 1, p. 6) the statement from 1946; it cannot be emphasized enough: "Like Fontenelle, I gave myself over to the fantasy of having my hand filled with truths all the better to hold on to them" ("Presentation on Psychical Causality," Lacan 2006b, 123). How can it be more obvious? To close one's hand around truths is a fantasy; to give oneself over to this is a dereliction of duty; and Lacan continues: "I confess that it is a ridiculous fantasy, marking, as it does, the limitations of a being who is on the verge of bearing witness" (ibid.).[11] One thus has to open up one's hands, that is, reveal, that is, speak and say the truth.

Especially since silence is, in the register of the real, impossible. This is how the prosopopoeia "I, truth, speak" should be understood ("The Freudian Thing," Lacan 2006e, 340: a text from 1955). With it, Fontenelle seems to be once and for all refuted: what good is it to have one's hands clasped over the truth if the truth speaks? One thinks of *Bijoux indiscrets*.[12] The truth's lack of discretion is proclaimed—is it an accident?—in Vienna, the city of Freud and Wittgenstein. In other words, Wittgenstein would be right, if only that of which one cannot speak agreed to remain silent. The point is that it does not agree to this. This is precisely what the unconscious is. So how can we agree not to speak about what does not shut up, however impossible our attempts are? And does it matter if we agree, when silence is impossible for the subject anyway?

Impossible to speak, impossible not to speak. Hence the in-between strategies, of *mi-dire*, of *pas-tout*. The aphorism "the truth does not all get said" does not mean that the truth is not said—it does say itself, but not-all. And, saying itself, even if not-all, it does not have to be shown. There are no tableaux of truth. The logic of the partial, the incomplete, the in-between, the *heteros*, fixes Wittgenstein's dichotomy: to say is to bring together what is radically foreign to itself.

Already in the first classicism's program, signifiers emerged from the clash between veiling and unveiling. Among the repeated commentaries that Lacan offered for fragment 18 of Heraclitus: "*oute legei oute kruptei, alla semainei*," we will highlight this one: "the Delphic god makes the signifier." As if signifiers, alone, were what allowed one to pass through the columns of Hercules, between saying and not saying. In the second classicism, the ethic of *bien dire* is posited as the symmetrical inverse of the *Tractatus*'s final thesis: "*Wovon man nicht sprechen kann, darüber muss man schweigen*," "Whereof one cannot speak, thereof one must be silent" (Wittgenstein 1998 [1921], 108). That there exist *x*'s about which one cannot speak, about which one must be silent, okay; assuming that there is any duty (*sollen*) here, the duty then is to *bien dire*.[13] But to *bien dire* is to bring together what cannot be brought together.

This heterology is all over the oeuvre. In its first form, the doctrine of the knot is just one version of it among others. Regarding the matheme, we've seen references to the Platonic *orthe doxa*, to the cross-cap, and to Russellian and anti-Russellian symbols. These are radically anti-Wittgensteinian arrangements. In the strict sense, they are situated on both sides of a limit that was understood to be real and impassable; this is what Wittgenstein had always ruled out: "in order to draw a limit to thinking we should have to be able to think both sides of this limit (we should therefore have to be able to think what cannot be thought)" (Wittgenstein 1998 [1921], 27). But, after all, what is the unconscious if not precisely a limit to the act of thinking, with respect to which psychoanalysis, from Freud on, aims to think both sides at once? In the deepest recesses of the Freudian object is found the real pulse to which the Lacanian *mi-dire* is the most faithful guarantor. If psychoanalysis is true, we must take the following two things to be in solidarity with each other: the *Spaltung* that splits the subject as thinking and is called the unconscious, and the heterology that both divides and stitches sayings back together. To renounce one is to renounce the other. With every display, the knot hindered *mi-dire* as a pathway to *bien dire*, but the hindering of *mi-dire* and the inaccessibility of *bien dire* are an abolition of the unconscious. If silence is not only required, but also possible ("you must be silent, therefore you can be"), it is because the truth does not speak and the unconscious does not exist. There is no Freudian thing. If Wittgenstein carries the day, if the knot carries the day over writing, Lacan is not the only one destroyed.

It would seem that a double renunciation, an abolition and a silence, took over. Would the Wittgenstein of the *Tractatus* then be the absolute Master? Would the tableaux that he shows turn him into the

Signorelli of thought? Or, beyond him, would Gorgias have triumphed against Socrates ("nothing exists; moreover, if anything did exist, it would be unknowable; moreover, if it did exist and were knowable, it would not be able to be shown to others")? Or Kripke's Wittgenstein, who perhaps nullifies the *cogito* and who is perhaps just a legend? Or ancient skepticism, which is perhaps also one?[14]

But this will not be my conclusion. I will only say that the second classicism underwent a decline. Like the first, it too perished. There is a core doctrinal reason for this event: the emergence of the knot. With almost machine-like efficiency, its emergence unmoored the agency of the letter; floating around like a drunken ship, it would proliferate indefinitely—flying the flag of Joyce. The program, then, is clear; after the end of the second classicism, just one problem remains: what is the relationship between the "it is shown" and "it is written" (incompatibility or not, equivalence or not)?

The solution was not developed; although it shows up briefly in some of the *Scripta* (in "Lituraterre," for example), the problem itself is just being stated here by one reader among others. He has not brought to a close the withdrawal of the second classicism. The needle is stuck between two positions. This just means that Lacan's oeuvre is incomplete. It is comparable in this respect, as I've said, to the great materialist oeuvres. *De natura rerum* ends with the plague of Athens; no one knows how Lucretius would have continued it; no one knows if we have lost what he wrote, or if he chose to remain silent, or if death forced his hand, or madness. Does this mean that the true nature of Venus is the death of all and the decay of each?[15]

No one can be sure what might have replaced the second classicism. But we can be sure that the second classicism was brought to completion, and that it was not the final word.

Afterword to the English Translation

L'Oeuvre claire was published in February 1996, by Seuil, in the collection *L'Ordre philosophique*. At the time, I was fully active in the area of my academic specialization; I adhered to the paradigm that Noam Chomsky and his school had developed, while also intending to fix what I wasn't satisfied with about it. A few years earlier, I had published a treatise in which I tried to define the general conditions that would allow linguistics to qualify as a Galilean science.[1] Now, it was quite obvious that in none of its versions was linguistics mathematized in the sense in which physics had been with Galileo. So, either linguistics was not a Galilean science, or else Galilean mathematization had to be understood in a less narrow sense than it had usually been. I chose the second position.

My reflections on linguistics had led me to reconsider the notion of a Galilean science. I could from then on undertake another task. As I pursued my work as a linguist, as I adopted a resolutely "scientistic" position, I wondered about Lacan's oeuvre. It had never ceased to be important for me even if, in the name of political militancy, I had to distance myself from it for five or six years after May 1968. After this interruption, I began to follow the seminars again; I read and reread the *Écrits*; I looked forward to the entire publication of the *Seminar*, which Jacques-Alain Miller had agreed to take on. Invited by the latter to the Department of Psychoanalysis of University Paris-VIII Vincennes, I gave a course in 1974–75 out of which I developed an article for the review *Ornicar?* and then a book entitled *L'Amour de la langue*.[2] What is more, Lacan, thanks to a few thoughtful gestures, led me to think that he was not indifferent to my work as a linguist; especially testifying to this was the fact that he had invited me to address a session of his seminar on April 10, 1973. Likewise, he was kind enough to give me some favorable remarks at the end of a talk I gave in September 1979, at the last congress of the École Freudienne de Paris.[3]

That being said, I could not avoid taking into account the scientistic choice which I had just imposed on myself regarding linguistic structure [*langue*] and language [*langage*]. Of course, I had already meditated on the position of the linguist; in *L'Amour de la langue* I had confronted it with the Lacanian orientation. I had at the same time located the differences that separate the two projects and set the conditions for putting them in relation to each other. But even while placing linguistics on the side of science, I had not then thought to strengthen my characterization of the latter. In my *Introduction à une science du language*, by contrast, I gave the ideal of science more precise characteristics. I had to establish whether the Lacanian reference to this ideal was affected by them.

From then on it was not only a matter of linguistics alone, but of science as such. By linking the birth of psychoanalysis to Freud's loyalty to the scientistic ideals of his day, was Lacan adhering to a historical thesis? "Koyré is our guide here," he had pronounced on December 1, 1965, in "Science and Truth," the first session of the seminars to be held at the École Normale Supérieure in the rue d'Ulm (Lacan 2006m, 727). As is often the case, the apparent simplicity of the phrase ["Koyré is our guide here"] must give us pause. Precisely because its syntax and wording are simple, the reader must be careful. Under the pretext of basing himself on a recognized authority, Lacan was setting up, between the lines, a theorem that needed to be made explicit, and whose consequences needed to be drawn out. In the title of his inaugural session, the word *science* served as shorthand for an entire doctrine. This doctrine came to dominate, for some time, an entire section of Lacan's oeuvre. It had to be brought to light as completely as possible. In order to do this, I adopted a model.

Among my own readings in scientism, I had felt the strongest admiration for the work of Ernst Mach on mechanics.[4] He carefully examines the theories of mechanics and especially Newtonian physics, such as Newton himself presented it. He clarifies its logical organization, to the point of detecting its lacunas, unfounded presuppositions, and even contradictions. I proposed to do the same with respect to Lacan.

One might think that I was putting him to the test; in fact, I was putting myself to the test: was my attachment to Lacan's oeuvre anything other than loyalty? Anything other than a refusal—a stubborn refusal to renounce something that had dazzled me as a youth? Moreover, was it self-evident that an oeuvre could even be spoken of in this particular case? If so, how was it constituted? A swarm of sub-questions emerged from the initial question.

Well, I came to a conclusion at the end of my work: Lacan held up. The notion of an oeuvre turned out to be fertile. What's more, my linguistic investigation bore fruit. By enlarging the criteria of Galilean science, I had equally been able to stabilize the relationship that Lacan established between it and psychoanalysis. Not only could the exact import of his references to Koyré and Kojève now be determined, not only could what constituted an oeuvre in his case be methodically defined, but, apart from occasional difficulties of expression, clarity reigned. Whence the title [*L'Oeuvre claire*] that came to me; it was not at all a provocation, even if it was going against a received idea. In order to prevent his reader from falling asleep, Lacan put obstacles in his path; conventional wisdom considers these to be obscurities. It is wrong, or rather, it is missing what is essential: whatever ornaments and veils complicate the writing of some phrases, the oeuvre is clear.

Today, more than two decades have passed. I uphold the validity of the method that I chose: the Euclidean presentation by means of axioms, theorems, and lemmas does not have to be privileged, but it has its advantages. It allows the important points of the discourse to be isolated though not without, when necessary, making breaks appear. Such that one benefits by recognizing areas of coherence that are both distinct and successive; in speaking of the first and second classicism, there is a gain in intelligibility. It goes without saying that the word "classicism" is neither laudatory nor pejorative; it signals, in a neutral manner, in the heart of the discourse, a momentary stabilization of relationships.

When I go back to the project that I formed in 1995, I find that it is still pertinent, and I have the sense that I basically accomplished what I set out to do. I thus have no problem with allowing my book, despite its age, to be made accessible, without modifications, to a new public. Nevertheless, no work is definitive. All the more so since textual conditions have changed. In 1995, Lacan's seminars only existed in two officially recognized forms:

(a) The volumes published by Seuil, in the collection *Champ freudien*; there were nine at the time. The first one to be published was also the most recent in the internal chronology of the seminar: Seminar XX, delivered in 1972–73 under the title *Encore* and published in 1975; all the other seminars published between 1975 and 1995 were prior to it. They were I, II, III, IV, VII, VIII, XI, and XVII.

(b) The regular transcriptions published in the review *Ornicar?* beginning with volume 2 (March 1975). The first seminar to be given this mode of transmission was XXII, entitled *R. S. I.*

Today, the situation has changed completely: the seminars are now, with the exception of a few volumes [*R. S. I.* among them], completely available in book form. Their texts have been edited with care. It could now be said that the *Seminar* constitutes an oeuvre in and of itself. If the notion of an oeuvre remains pertinent, Lacan's oeuvre is thus present in a different form compared to 1995. And we are now justified in asking if there does not exist an "oral Lacan," distinct from the "written Lacan" of the *Scripta*. According to this hypothesis, each of the two branches would be as important as the other, with each possessing its own characteristics.

If we admit that *A Search for Clarity* assumed the right to consider only the "written Lacan," this choice is not necessarily thrown into question.

On the contrary, it could be preserved, and we could make a complementary choice about the "oral Lacan"; a new project would take shape: consider only the "oral Lacan"; study its development; note the echo effects or modulations that sometimes appear in it with respect to the "written Lacan," but without treating it as if it were dependent on the "written Lacan." In 1995, I leaned on the distinction between the esoteric and exoteric; I detected protreptic effects in the *Seminar*; I do not see any reason to renounce this approach. However, the hypothesis itself must still be examined closely: is there an autonomous and self-sufficient "oral Lacan"? Two opposed answers are possible. And as long as the foundations and consequences of each have not been assessed, adopting any position on the matter would be precarious. Let's just say that in 2020, *A Search for Clarity*'s bias is neither confirmed nor denied by the evolution of the Lacanian corpus.

Moreover, Lacan continued to publish texts after 1973. And he modified how he wrote. Linguistic games became an essential part of the machinery. They were no longer just frequent; they were constant. They played a major role in transmission. In this sense, they did more than contribute to what Lacan called the *matheme*. They were its statistically dominant form. This movement ended with a reference to Joyce. Beginning with *Seminar XXIII, Le Sinthome* (1975–76), this occupied a more and more important place, to the point that it is justifiable to speak of a Joycean turn in the oeuvre.

The fact is that *A Search for Clarity* does not take this Joycean turn into account. The last chapter, entitled "The Deconstruction," alludes to it. Passages from Seminars XXII and XXIV are commented on in this chapter; what is said of them is not false, but fails to grasp the scale of the event. For a long time, in fact, I even denied that there had been an event. I argued to myself that the publication of Seminar XX in the form of a volume, with Lacan's consent, had brought about a break. This seminar developed a new doctrine of the letter, as well as the foundational elements for the topology of knots. I concluded that it was justifiable to see in it the opening of a decisive period. The seminars prior to Seminar XX could all the more readily be set aside, given that Lacan had generally chosen to get their substance across in the form of articles. As for the later seminars, I was not unaware of them, but according to me, they were limited to developing the implications of Seminar XX; although I maintained at the time that the process would take the form of a deconstruction. In other words, I assumed that after Seminar XX, there would not be another break. I noted the obvious discursive changes in the later seminars, but they did not shake my conviction; I attributed them to the internal instabilities of the doctrine of the knot, and the aftereffects they had on the doctrines of the letter and the matheme.

One aspect of my reasoning can be preserved. I maintain that the consequences that follow from the expansion of a published corpus must not be exaggerated. Without necessarily backtracking on the notion of the oeuvre, I continue to judge it appropriate to distinguish between written teaching and oral teaching. Among the texts in print, it makes sense to treat the writings intended from the beginning for publication in a specific manner. They should be separated from transcribed texts whose publication was often decided *après coup* and sometimes belatedly. Even if one does not go so far as to see the *Seminar* as an oeuvre in itself, as an "oral Lacan" parallel to the "written Lacan," it makes sense to consider it on its own, without seeing it merely as the preparatory work for one or several writings. Among the published volumes, Seminar XX keeps its singularity, if only for having, in the eyes of Lacan himself, inaugurated a new phase in the relationship between the oral and the written. On this point as well, the organization that I outlined in *A Search for Clarity* retains some of its pertinence; the status of oral teaching certainly changed once it could benefit almost immediately from reliable transcriptions, but this rapid turnover does not necessarily affect the status of written teaching.

But from this it does not follow that I can maintain the conservative position that I had held for too long. Contrary to what I had thought, events did happen, after Seminar XX, which fundamentally changed things. For me to be convinced of this, for me, according to the Kantian expression, to have been awakened from my dogmatic slumbers, the reading of one book counted more than others. While acquainting myself with Éric Laurent's *L'Envers de la biopolitique*[5] I made two discoveries. The first was about Jacques-Alain Miller's teaching. I was aware of its value, but in order for a school to exist, it is not enough that it contain valid knowledge; it is also necessary that this knowledge allows for the production of new knowledge.

Freud never gave way on this point; he was constantly looking into the publications of those who claimed to be his followers, in order to see if they were going beyond pure and simple conformity. We know that he was often disappointed by innovators, but he never stopped expecting an essential contribution from them. Besides, the irony of circumstances made it the case that as far as a proof of his teaching's force goes, the best testimony for it came to him after his death, from a place and a language from which he expected nothing; having renounced German, he had put all of his hopes into English. The French language, and Paris, which had meant so much to him prior to 1900, had disappointed him.

But in 1964, Lacan and the École Freudienne de Paris vouched, almost single-handedly, for the future of Freudianism. If Lacan used the word *school* at the time in order to designate the institution that he founded, this should not be seen as an arbitrary preference but as a decisive choice. For there to be a school, there must be students; a student—in contrast to a disciple—is ascertained in only one way: when what he learns in the school gives rise to something new. All I had to do was look around in order to be convinced that Lacan's teaching had the requisite fecundity. Whether at the Department of Psychoanalysis at Paris-VIII or at the École de la Cause Freudienne, Jacques-Alain Miller's activity would have been enough to bring about my conclusion: new knowledge was being formulated on the basis of Lacan. But did this first layer of new knowledge give rise to students who, on its basis, were able to create a second layer of new knowledge? I did not doubt this in principle, but it took reading Éric Laurent's book for me to experience it.

Another discovery followed the first one: reading, line by line, the text and the notes of *L'Envers de la biopolitique,* I realized that I had totally misrecognized the nature and importance of the Joycean turn. In no way did it have to be reduced to a deconstruction; quite the contrary, it had to be understood in positive terms. In no way should it have been treated as a response to the possible difficulties of the doctrine of the knot; quite the contrary, it had to be considered something autonomous, the discovery of a new continent. After the break that was Seminar XX, other breaks were produced; the oeuvre and name of Joyce signaled one among them, and without a doubt the most important one. I could not then deny the existence and magnitude of my misrecognition. This involved much more than the faults of inattention. It had to be diagnosed as a resistance, in the proper sense of the word.

I resisted homophony. Whereas I believed I had taken its exact measure, I was missing an essential dimension of it. I had rendered myself deaf to what was emerging in the *Seminar,* such as it was transcribed in *Ornicar?* session after session, starting in 1975. I had remained indifferent to the developments that the oeuvre and life of Joyce brought about in Seminar XXIII. I was dismissive of "La Troisième," in 1975 as well as in 2011.[6] But these false steps ran into one and the same stumbling block: homophony.[7]

I had every reason not to become aware of it. In fact, I had continually meditated on homophony and *lalangue.* Since *L'Amour de la langue* I had emphasized the impossibility that these had for the linguist. I had tried to demonstrate that in Saussure, the promotion of *la langue* [linguistic structure] (in two words) to the detriment of language found its inverted image in the research into anagrams; this work, long ignored, materialized a return of *lalangue* (in a single word) in the linguist's activity, both as a scholar and a subject. Almost alone in the global university, Jakobson had been excited by this discovery. Having worked with him on his analysis of Baudelaire, I carried out, under his direction, the manipulation of phonemes thanks to which he endeavored to revolutionize poetics.[8] Even in *A Search for Clarity* I put forward declarations that could lead one to believe that they were doing justice to the Joycean turn. For example, in chapter 5: "The homonymical puns that are developed in Lacan's remarks starting from the 1970s are not witticisms; they are detached from any *Witz*; one by one they form a literal cellule, an atom of poematic calculus. . . . At first able to be thought of as completely homomorphic to mathematical letters (it is in this sense that, in 'L'Étourdit,' when the matheme is introduced, the homophonic play is already present, starting with the title itself), they are like mathemes produced by *lalangue* itself."[9] Or: "Each of the homophonic games, in the titles of the seminars, in the written elaborations, in the incessant return to Joyce, is like a pod containing within itself the possibility of a letter coming from language alone, entirely different from what mathematics . . . proposed—and yet given identical functions."[10]

But make no mistake. Even though it seems like the essentials are being said here, nothing is being said about them. In fact, it suffices to put these extracts back into their context in order to note that homophony remains subordinated; homophony reduces the effects of what I call the deconstruction of the matheme, but it does not modify the nature of the process. When I wrote that homophonies "are like mathemes," I meant between the lines that they partially compensate for the fragility of the authentic mathemes. But it is much rather the case that, henceforth, the homophonies *are* the matheme par excellence. They are the means of its transmissibility. They incarnate the violence and efficacity of literality, more purely than Bourbakist letters do. *Lalangue* is not just a milieu in which what is heard is refracted in what is said; it has become active; one can draw a force from it that is able to open points of passage for sense.

So something happened with respect to homophony. The version of it that I had for so long accepted we can call *given* homophony. Given by the happenstance that Lacan, in *Television*, called "the good luck of lalangue" [*le bon heur de lalangue*], making sure that the dimension of luck [*heur*], which can be equally good or bad, was isolated.[11] The anagram, the pun, the slip, the *poème*, I did not at all ignore these games, and I practiced some of them. When Victor Hugo describes puns as "the droppings of soaring wit," he joins up with the logic of the gift as Freud had formulated it: "poo is the first gift." *Lalangue* gives homophonies to the subject; homophonies, quite often, provide us with our first encounters with *lalangue.* Should we be surprised that children are spurred on by echoing repetitions: *papa, mama, dada,* etc.? Something other than language as a faculty of speaking, or language as the order of "say this, but don't say that," is at work here. We can explain why certain consonants or vowels are preferred; Jakobson applied himself to this task successfully.[12] But this does not suffice; the return of the Same also has to be accounted for, whether it is found in rhymes, in refrains, or in slogans: homophony exerts a power over speaking beings. The gift can be made into a means of action. Propaganda and advertising have known how to make use of this. All the more reason not to let them monopolize it. Otherwise *lalangue* becomes a machine for servitude.

From the 1970s, Lacan is no longer content with homophonies that are just given. He will no longer confine himself to the games that find language and *lalangue* amusing but leave them unchanged. After all, Heine's "Famillionär," made famous by Freud, was not meant to transform the German language; quite the contrary. It was limited to adding up two given and reciprocal homophonies, one that goes from *familiär* to *Millionär* and one that goes from *Millionär* to *familiär.* When Lacan in the seminar on "The Purloined Letter" scoffed at "*la politique de l'autruiche,*" he adds *autrui* and *autruche,* not without perhaps alluding to Austria's blindness, for which it paid the price in 1938 and whose consequences Freud, with thousands of others, suffered.[13] Neither language nor *lalangue* bear any scars from it. By contrast, the artifacts of *Finnegans Wake* aim to dislocate the English language and, in fact, any possible human language. Out of immediate homophonies they make more secret homophonies, born of the former. Beyond addition many other operations are used, such that it is often impossible to affirm with certitude whether all of the homophonies involved in a segment of the text have been detected. If it is right to consider immediate homophonies as givens, these second homophonies are in fact constructed by Joyce himself; they are not gifts, but the spoils of war.

David Hayman highlighted the insistent presence of Mallarmé and *A Throw of the Dice* in *Finnegans Wake.*[14] However, nothing about what is read or heard is left to chance; everything is the result of a strategy of abolition. We are no longer dealing with what offers itself up. Rather, a conquest is called to mind: using all the languages of the world, but also all the knowledge that can be spoken, Joyce pulls homophonies out of English *lalangue* that it does not give.

In a similar manner, Lacan's artifacts call for a more and more attentive examination so that particular homophonic facets are not overlooked. When, on the first page of "Joyce le Symptôme," the word *escabeau* [stepladder] appears in relation to LOM, it is preceded and followed by variations based on both phonemes and orthography;[15] Lacan thus makes homophonies that go beyond those that *lalangue* offers directly, or that can be obtained by simple operations.[16] From these more complex manipulations unexpected meaning-effects arise. Here is an example: the rhyme between *escabeau/beau* is easily heard, without it catching the speaking subject's attention at first. But even before *escabeau* is mentioned, Lacan rewords it as *hissecroibeau*; the ear hears "*il se croit beau*" [he fancies himself beautiful], *il* losing the final /l/ before the consonant, as is often the case. As a result, when *escabeau* does appear, the presence of *beau* retroactively ceases to be anodyne. The homophony between *escabeau/beau* [stepladder/beautiful] was given by language, but for such a brief moment that the crystal of *lalangue* did not refract any of its brightness. Thanks to the detour by a homophony not given by language, a new facet on the crystal shines forth. Moreover, the artifact begins with an /h/; the ear does not perceive it, but the eye decodes the verb *hisser* [to hoist, to pull up]; the Beautiful is not only brought forth by rhyme with *escabeau*, but becomes the effect of a movement from the ground up. At the heart of the word *escabeau* we find the Freudian doctrine on the upright position; Freud noted that it separated the high part of the body, reserved for thought, from the sexual parts, situated below. He added that art does not give any aesthetic value to the latter, whereas the face, raised [*hissé*] to the summit of the anatomy, was destined to conform to the requirements of the Beautiful; in connection with this he cites Napoleon, and for the first time in his work he states that "anatomy is destiny."[17] In Lacan's writing, the homophony that is given is not even mentioned; in the proper sense, it goes without saying. It only exists in order to allow for the conquering homophony, engulfed in a swarm of senses. Let's add that the presence of *hisse* assumes that the first operation is accomplished, the one that makes "*il se croit beau*" appear to the ear. Thus we have to do here with a successive sequence of conquering homophonies that give substance, *après coup*, to the homophony that is given.

When making *famillionär*, Heine started from the homophonies given by language, and then stopped. With Joyce and Lacan, the conquering homophonies can give rise to other conquering homophonies, without anyone being able to determine where it all stops. In the case of *escabeau/beau*, we can even say that the rhyme accedes to the level of homophony under the effect of the conquering homophony. During the Joycean turn, the homophonies are thus important *insofar as they are not given*; they lead the French language, but also French *lalangue*, to where they would not go if left to themselves. They tear them away from their immobility. Or to use Aristotle's terminology, they exert on *lalangue* a forced motion that takes it out of its natural location. They thus open up the paths of transmissibility.

Now, since *L'Amour de la langue* I had only paid attention to homophonies that are given; I neglected the conquering homophonies. I will be honest: I treated them with contempt. So it was true that I had lent an ear to homophony, but not to every kind. Conversely, I had not resisted every homophony, but I had resisted the ones that were promoted by the Joycean turn. In *Television* Lacan suggests that he thinks it is insufficient to rely on luck [*bon heur*] in *lalangue*, but that's what I stuck with. I went so far as to consider that Lacan's Joycean manipulations did not respect the rules of the game. They turned them into means, and subordinated them, I thought to myself, to an artificial fabrication. I could justify the procedure in the name of haste; in "La Troisième," Lacan mentions his possible death. By combining lexical unities that authorize three, four, or five levels of reading, he privileges an art of writing that frees itself from linearity. Like a Chinese ideogram, with which an analogy was drawn at the time, the homophonic artifact can suggest several significations at once. In a race against time, it allows for victory. This justification mitigated my lack of esteem for the Joycean manipulations; it did not abolish it.

There's more. The Joycean turn even brought about a change in homophonies that are given. Again in "La Troisième" Lacan is explicit about them:

> Lalangue is what makes it possible to consider that it is not purely by chance [*hazard*] that *voeu*, a wish, is also *veut*, third person indicative of *vouloir*; nor is it by chance either that the negating *non* should also be the naming *nom*; nor is it by chance, or arbitrary, as Saussure said, that *d'eux*, *d* in front of *eux* designating those [*ceux*] of whom we speak, should be made in the same way as the number two, *deux*. What must be appreciated is the deposit, the alluvium, the petrification by which it is marked, through the way a group handles its unconscious experience.[18]

The decisive phrase here is "it is not purely by chance." We must be clear: it strips luck of what was essential about its importance. But in my relationship to homophonies I privileged the element of chance. I readily cited Mallarmé on this subject. Lacan, it still seems to me today, had for a long time followed this path too, but from 1975 on he took another route. Not only does he set chance aside, but he begins a reflection on the relationship between the collective and the unconscious. Where can this reflection go? I feel unable at this point to determine it more precisely, but it is important to me that the question be asked, and that it be asked regarding *lalangue*. The Lacanian orientation thus establishes a research program for itself. I would be happy to take part in it, but it is out of the question that I work on it alone.

I have wondered about the reasons for my misrecognition. I was paying the price for my status as a freelance researcher. I had belonged to the École Freudienne de Paris; I could feel that I was a student of Lacan, at a distance whose principle Lacan himself accepted. However, this material distance was aggravated to the point that it changed into isolation—a "wall of ice," Lacan murmured one day. This situation made me independent. But it also led me to blunder; not just once, no doubt, but at least once. I botched the Joycean turn. My autonomy changed into autarchy and my autarchy into penury.

Left to my own devices, I was not able to triumph over my resistance to homophony as it is situated in "La Troisième." If only for one reason: when it is disjoined from chance, homophony is as unthinkable and unimaginable for the linguist as the resurrection of the flesh was for ancient philosophers.

In these conditions, the status of *A Search for Clarity* changes. Far from grasping the entirety of Lacan's trajectory, the work must be thought of as partial. But rather than seeing this as a fault, we can say that this is where we find its value. It shows how far a reading can go when it only takes into account homophonies that are given, and when they are entirely attributed to chance. In this sense, we have here a thought experiment. By way of contrast, it allows us to better understand the stakes involved in the presence of Joyce. On this basis, the art of writing used by Lacan in his last texts can be better analyzed.

As I have already noted, it is entirely justified once it has been understood that Lacan was in a race against time. The function of haste appeared already in March 1945; at the time it was part of a collective logic. Thirty years later, it took on a vital importance. Since the clock was ticking, Lacan sped up his speech in order to overtake the absolute master, death. But perhaps Leo Strauss should also be thought of here. Thanks to the homophonies that conquer, the careful reader detects meanings that he did not expect, bearing on themes whose presence is surprising. I mean properly political themes. I insist, for example, that "Joyce le symptôme" includes, among its layers of meaning, the elements for a politics of the rights of man.[19] Between the homophonies that are given and the homophony that conquers, a chasm has to be crossed. *A Search for Clarity* can help with this, precisely because the text testifies to a real, in the form of a resistance to this real. Rereading it has been beneficial to me, and I thank Ed Pluth for giving me the opportunity. It may be that reading it will be useful to others.

Notes

Introduction

1. [Milner is alluding here to the title of Martial Gueroult's influential multivolume work on Descartes, *Descartes's Philosophy Interpreted according to the Order of Reasons* (Gueroult 1984 [1953]). —*Trans.*]

Chapter 1

1. In this chapter the word "culture" will be used consistently in the French sense and not in the sense of *Kultur*.

2. I am deliberately setting aside the question of the university here. It is a nontrivial matter to know whether the professional productions of academics (theses, memoirs, etc.) fall under the oeuvre form. The French tradition says yes; the German or English says no. This obviously does not mean that all French theses (I am speaking of theses in the ancient sense) are oeuvres, nor does it mean that no German or English ones are.

3. [In French, the word *Cours* can be either singular or plural: the English translation opts for the singular. —*Trans.*]

4. Nothing demonstrates the strictly formal character of the notion of the oeuvre better than this. The title of the *Course* equivocates between the singular and the plural; it was not given by Saussure; the text was worked over to the point that not one of its pages can be attributed as is to Saussure's hand; and Saussure never had the intention of publishing any course. Nevertheless, there is an oeuvre and, therefore, an author, because the formal criteria are met. See J.-C. Milner, "Retour à Saussure," in *Le Périple structural* (Lagrasse, Fr.: Verdier/poche, 2008 [2002]), 15–43.

5. On May 25, 1913, at the first meeting of the IPA committee, Freud offered to each of his five collaborators a Greek intaglio that they wore as rings. Freud himself wore a similar ring and, in 1920, a new member received the same gift. So there were seven rings altogether. Those involved, and Freud himself, knew how fanciful this behavior was. See Jones 1955, 174–75. Internationalism, rings, Greece, childishness: a reference to Coubertin is not out of place. [Pierre de Coubertin, 1863–1937, France, was the founder of the International Olympic Committee. —*Trans.*]

6. [Bernard de Fontenelle, 1657–1757, French writer and philosopher. –*Trans.*]

7. [In his translation of Lacan's *Seminar XX*, where this word appears, Bruce Fink explains: "*Poubellication* is a condensation of *poubelle*, garbage can (or dustbin) and *publication*, publication" (Lacan 1998 [1975], 26, note 2). –*Trans.*]

8. [Latin phrase meaning "flesh given over to worms": the beginning letters of each word create the word "cadaver." –*Trans.*]

9. [The word *poublier*, adding an "o" to the verb *publier* (to publish), links publishing with the forgotten (*oublier*: to forget). –*Trans.*]

10. When the relevant documents are read, there is no doubt that there was a decision and that it was explicit. See Lacan 1990b (1977), 53–80. It is less certain that it was as ecclesiastical in style as it was said to be at the time. Lacan (*Seminar XI*, Lacan 1978 [1973], 3) refers to a major excommunication, but this just highlights the difference: the Church of Rome does not proclaim excommunication without any hope for return. He then mentions the *Schammatha* pronounced by the synagogue of Amsterdam against Spinoza, which did add the impossibility of return. But there is not, and could not be, a universal synagogue. One could equally mention *The Scarlet Letter*, but there is not an international Calvinist church either. Once again, the different international boards that rule global entertainment, at once all-powerful and frivolous, are called to mind.

11. [Jacques Attali, 1943–present, French economist, writer, adviser to Mitterrand after his 1981 election to the French presidency. –*Trans.*]

12. [La Bibliothèque de la Pléiade (The Pleaides Library) is an imprint of the publishing house Gallimard, and was created in 1931 to produce standard editions of classical works. –*Trans.*]

13. In 1964 Lacan himself brought to my attention the short book in which J. Bidez presented the works of W. Jaeger and E. Bignone to the Francophone public (*Un singulier naufrage littéraire dans l'antiquite: A la recherche des épaves de l'Aristote perdu* [Brussels: Collection Lebègue, 1943]). Moreover, it seems that W. Jaeger and Lacan maintained a correspondence.

14. Lacan developed a technique that could be called a "negative protreptics": its goal was to incite the subject to tear himself away from *doxa* by chastising him. The technique is not new: the Cynics practiced it, and it can be found in Lewis Carroll when dear sweet Alice, that likeable but dull bearer of the most Victorian of opinions, gets continually insulted by the representatives of *nonsense* [this is in English in the original. –*Trans.*], which is a symptom of the real; we find it, finally, in the surrealists and in Groucho Marx.

15. See the introduction to "The Instance of the Letter" (Lacan 2006f, 412), where Lacan presents his own text as "halfway" between writing and speech. It is worth noting, however, that the text arose as a *talk* requested by the FGEL in 1957. [The FGEL was a student organization. In the bibliographical references at the back of the *Écrits* the group is identified as the "Fédération des étudiants ès Lettres" (Lacan 2006, 866). –*Trans.*]

16. [Macrobius Ambrosius Theodosius, a fifth-century A.D. Roman whose *Commentary on the Dream of Scipio* was an important reference for Platonists in the

Middle Ages. François de La Mothe Le Vayer, 1588–1672, French writer, and tutor to Louis XIV. –*Trans.*]

17. Of course, one thinks of Montaigne here. The name Diderot equally comes to mind, who was one of the rare people, in France at least, to have used digression in his novels; he was also one of the rare moderns to have written great dialogues, not out of an indebtedness to Plato, but out of sheer invention and brilliance. When reading a seminar by Lacan, one catches oneself finding in it the accents of something like the *Rêve de d'Alembert*, except that all that is left are the replies by d'Alembert and Bordeu, mixed into one single text, while the audience—silent, or nearly so—would be in the position of poor Lespinasse, whose existence is only preserved thanks to the snubs that are directed at her.

18. [Gaëtan Gatian de Clérambault, 1872–1934, French psychiatrist with whom Lacan studied. Dr. du Boulbon is the doctor who takes care of the narrator's grandmother in Proust's *In Search of Lost Time*, and was a great admirer of the writer Bergotte. –*Trans.*]

19. Lacan's style thus consists of following the functional markers of proteptics and complete transmission. F. Regnault has proposed a typology more "intrinsic" to the structure of doctrine (Regnault 1992, 219–30). The difference in method leads to interesting differences in the results.

20. The American edition from 1952 of *Persecution and the Art of Writing* is cited in "The Instance of the Letter" (Lacan 2006f, 423), a text from 1957.

21. Whence the result that a written work following these rules (which are assumed to be ancient and forgotten) must appear to a modern person as a disordered hodgepodge of uninteresting propositions, all the more so the more important the oeuvre is. The argument here is an argument from authority: an ancient oeuvre, famous in antiquity, cannot have become famous for bad reasons; so if it appears uninteresting and poorly constructed to us, this must be because we are reading it poorly, or, more exactly, carelessly. Reciprocally, no truly important ancient oeuvre can have gone misrecognized, because careful readers once existed. The modern author, for his part, can hope for such readers, but he cannot be sure that they exist. Usually, he will have to assume that they do not. At the same time, he always writes under the condition of the misrecognized oeuvre. Lacan, from this point of view, is certainly modern.

22. [In the English translation of *Television*, the phrase *bien dire* is translated as "well-spoken." See Lacan 1990a (1973), 22. *Mi-dire* can be translated as "half-said." –*Trans.*]

23. In principle an exhaustive inventory of the *logia* could be made. There must also exist botched *logia*. They would have the right syntactical form, but the anticipated certitude that marks them was deferred up to the last moment. In the register of logical time, this is a movement forever suspended. A sign that we are dealing with one of these is when Lacan does not return to it once it was emitted; this is what gives them an enigmatic status. However, there is no legitimate place for enigmas in Lacan. If there are in fact enigmas, they are the signs of an impasse. I suggest as an example the command "do not give way on your desire," which some have thought to be able to extract from Seminar VII.

24. Seminar XX, which is at the height of Lacan's second classicism, is an exception to which we will have to return (see chapter 5, p. 107–8). It comes close to canceling out the difference between the esoteric and exoteric—or, what amounts to the same thing, it often abandons the protreptic style.

25. [Alain, pseudonym of Émile Chartier, 1868–1951, a philosopher who exerted a deep influence on many future students of the École Normale Supérieure. Jules Lagneau, 1851–1894, was Alain's mentor in philosophy. Charles-Marc Des Granges, 1861–1944, author, editor. Ferdinand Brunetière, 1849–1906, literary critic. – Trans.]

26. Read Detienne on this point: *The Masters of Truth in Archaic Greece* (Cambridge, Mass.: Zone, 1999), but not without clarifying it by a reading of Roubaud's *L'Invention du fils de Leoprepes* (Paris: Circé, 1993).

Chapter 2

1. This is formulated explicitly in "Science and Truth," Lacan 2006m, 743.

2. I am referring to F. Regnault's book *Dieu est inconscient* (Paris: Navarin, 1985); his talk at the École de la Cause on October 15, 1989, "Entre Ferdinand and Léopold," should be added as well. [This was reprinted as "Traits de genie" in *Connaissez-vous Lacan?* ed. M.-P. de Cossé-Brissac et al. (Paris: Seuil, 1992), 219–30. – Trans.]. These works make it unnecessary to refer to any others on this matter, if they exist.

3. Someday someone will have to explain by what sleight of hand the word "scientism" has become an insult. In my eyes it is not one; no more than the words "materialism," "atheism," or "irreligion" are, for example (I give these here randomly). Lacan constantly relates Freud to scientism (see especially "Science and Truth," Lacan 2006m, 727–29). Even if Lacan were trying to establish how he differs from Freud when he used the word "scientism," it does not seem that he used it to belittle the one to whom he wanted to return.

4. The disjunction-conjunction of the ideal of science and the ideal science was introduced in *Cahiers pour l'Analyse*, vol. 9. Obviously, it correlates to the disjunction-conjunction of the ego ideal and the ideal ego, as Lacan articulates it on the basis of D. Lagache's work in his "Remarks on Daniel Lagache's Presentation: 'Psychoanalysis and Personality Structure'" (Lacan 2006h, 543–74: see especially 562–72). The illusory effects that are at work in and around the word *science* can easily be deduced from such a structural analogy. They exist, they must be dissipated, but science is not reducible to them.

5. One fact among others: in 1911 Freud co-signed a manifesto calling for the creation of a society that would develop and diffuse a positivist philosophy. Among the signatories we find the names of E. Mach, D. Hilbert, F. Klein, and A. Einstein. There are two important things about this: the fact that Freud signed it says something about his views when he was publishing the third edition of the *Traumdeutung* and had just founded the IPA and the *Zentralblatt fur Psychoanalyse;* and moreover, considering the amount of vetting that usually accompanies such an affair, the fact that Freud's name was accepted, and perhaps even solicited, tells

us about his standing within the German-language positivist milieu. On this point, see the important historical introduction by A. Soulez to the collection *Manifeste du cercle de Vienne et autres écrits* (Paris: Presses Universitaires de France, 1985), 32.

6. [Also in Lacan 2001b (1965), 187. – *Trans.*]

7. [Ten volumes of the *Cahiers pour l'Analyse* were published between 1966 and 1969, and Milner was one of the journal's founding editors. All ten volumes can be found online at http://cahiers.kingston.ac.uk/. – *Trans.*]

8. Kojève himself, in "L'Origine chrétienne de la science modern" (in *Mélanges Alexandre Koyré: L'Aventure de l'ésprit*, vol. 2 [Paris: Hermann, 1964], 295–306), articulates a proposition similar to this, but it does seem that Lacan was first, since he formulated his hypothesis after 1960. Moreover, it is not certain that the two propositions mean exactly the same thing. See the following note.

9. See Lacan's seventh seminar: "modern science, the kind that was born with Galileo, could only have developed out of biblical or Judaic ideology, and not out of ancient philosophy or the Aristotelian tradition" (Lacan 1992 [1986], 122). Here we see what separates Kojève from Lacan; Kojève gives Christianity and more particularly the doctrine of the Incarnation (Kojève 1964, 303) a decisive role in the emergence of science; but this dogma is precisely what separates Christianity from Judaism, and justifies Christianity's claim that it adheres to the spirit rather than the letter; Lacan gives a decisive role to Judaism and to what, in Christianity, is still Judaic—that is, precisely, letters. This means that Lacan's hypothesis (1960) does not overlap with Kojève's (1964), although they are almost homonyms.

10. Of course, Lacan's commentary relies heavily on Gueroult's instantaneist interpretation of Descartes. But not entirely, and Gueroult could be refuted on this point without Lacan's rewriting becoming completely invalidated (see J.-M. Beyssade, *La Philosophie première de Descartes* [Paris: Flammarion, 1979]). In the same manner, the reading is not ruled out by the fact that Descartes, in the *Meditations*, does not take up again how the *Discourse on Method* or the *Principles* formulated it: "I think, therefore I am," "*Cogito, ergo sum*" (see É. Balibar, "*Ego sum, ego existo*: Descartes on the Verge of Heresy," 2017, a talk given to the Société Francaise de Philosophie on February 22, 1992). We could even say that Lacan's rewriting follows the letter of the *Meditations* quite strictly: "this proposition: *I am* . . ."

11. [*Ça pense* in French. In this phrase, "it" should not be understood to be the unconscious itself as some new sort of thinking substance, but should be taken more generically and indefinitely, similar to how "it" is used in phrases like "it is raining" or "how's it going?" – *Trans.*]

12. And the coherence of the texts as well. Because there is an apparent contradiction, opposing the letter of Freud to the letter of Lacan: Freud posits that what is specific to the dreamwork, insofar as it is a major form of the unconscious, is that it does not think (*The Interpretation of Dreams*, Freud 1953b [1900], 507); Lacan posits that what is specific to the unconscious, and to the dream as one of its forms, can be summarized by the statement "it thinks." We can add to this the contradiction in which Freud is opposed to himself, when he sometimes affirms that the dream is a form of thought and sometimes affirms that it does

not think (ibid., 507). All of this can be cleared up, however. The thinking that Freud denies to the unconscious is a thinking with qualities; the thinking that he grants to it and by which Lacan defines it is a thinking without qualities. The *cogito* is necessary for this.

For Freud, to say that thinking is not part of the dreamwork is to say that the latter does not have the *modalities* of thinking: hypothesis-forming and judgment ("the dream-work . . . does not think, calculate, or judge in any way at all" (ibid., 507). That is, everything which allows for a *qualitative* distinction between opposed poles. We can compare the text of the *Traumdeutung* to that of the *Meditations*: Descartes holds that a thing which thinks is a thing that doubts, understands, affirms, denies, wills, refuses, and also imagines or senses; essential to this analysis is its differential character, which is not only able to distinguish among modalities but, within these, their poles (affirming/denying, etc.). If the dreamwork is what Freud says it is, then, according to this analysis, it is not the work of a thing that thinks. If, on the contrary, we say that the dream is a form of thinking, then it must be admitted that thinking happens even in cases when the differences between doubt and certainty, affirmation and negation, willing and refusing, imagination and sensation are problematic, if not altogether called into question. Freud, who was still a bit reserved when he was writing the *Traumdeutung* (whose final edition dates from 1911), will be explicit about this point in the article on negation (Freud 1964 [1925]): there is thinking, even where there are no polarities—and thus, no qualities. It could be the case that for Freud this thinking without qualities is ruled by the laws of quantity (energetics) alone. We'll see that signifiers will suggest that there are non-qualitative laws, which, however, will not be quantitative either. (See chapter 3, p. 57 and chapter 4, p. 88.)

From a more general point of view, it remains an open question whether the thinking without qualities, such as it is described here, is also a thinking without properties. It could be the case that it has "minimal" properties. Again, the theory of signifiers will give a specific answer to this question.

13. H. von Helmholtz had already in 1855 explicitly raised the question of a thought without self-consciousness ("*ein Denken ohne Selbstbewusstsein*"); see Helmholtz 1884 (1855), "Über das Sehen des Menschen," in *Vorträge und Reden*, vol. 1 (Braunschweig: Vieweg und Sohn), 390. This shows how scientism and the unconscious are historically linked. More precisely, by introducing a theory of the unconscious Freud does not separate himself from scientism: he fulfills its program.

14. [The French words *littéralisable, littéralisation, littéral* should be taken to be referring primarily to letters and the functioning and/or presence of letters, and not in the conventional sense of "literal" in English, as, for example, opposed to the metaphorical. As this group of words is used by Milner throughout this book, the key idea involves a production of or manipulation of letters, a rendering into letters . . . or, for example, a science that "has to do with letters"; thus, a *literalized* science, a science that *literalizes*, and so on is a science that uses letters (and not only numbers). All appearances of and variants on the word "literal" in this text are to be understood in this sense. –*Trans.*]

15. P. Redondi (1987, 57–65) argues that Galileo was an atomist. On this

point he is opposed to Koyré, who makes Galileo out to be a Platonist (1977 [1939], 201–98). Of course, the two interpretations are not necessarily incompatible (see F. Hallyn, *Le Sens des forms,* 1994, 296–97).

16. To be exact, I must emphasize that the link between precision and literality is not explicit in Koyré. Despite its historical importance I am setting aside the discussion of Bacon, in whose work the paradigm of the literal remains important, but is applied to cryptography rather than philology. Among the memorable encounters between philology and modern science, the correspondence between R. Bentley (the scholarly editor of Horace) and Newton must be cited (see A. Koyré, *Newtonian Studies,* 1965, 201–11). On the distinction between the "experimental" and the "instrumental," see G. Simon, *Le Regard, l'être, et l'apparence dans l'optique de l'antiquité* (Paris: Le Seuil, 1988), 201. According to this author, ancient optics was experimental; it was not and could not have been instrumental.

17. [See chapter 2, note 14. –*Trans.*]

18. The factual situation is of course much more complicated: is there an exact synonymy between science and the theory of technology, between technology and applied science? This is open to debate, just as it is debatable whether we find the same thing when we go "from right to left" from science to technology, or in going "from left to right" from technology towards science. Even today, with a mixture of fear and hope, we see that by bringing together research into biology and the discovery of vaccines, science is being made into a theorized technology, pure and simple. It is as free as one likes with respect to the objects it theorizes, but it must, however, have the following as its object: not Nature, but nature treated by technology; namely, not the configurations of molecules but these configurations insofar as they are modifiable by intentional procedures for the purposes of medical treatment. The controversy has become fierce regarding AIDS. An increasing number of researchers affirm that a vaccine will only be found by not searching for it. This implies that funding for research should go elsewhere, not to the search for the vaccine. This is strict Koyré, but people with AIDS have a hard time adhering to it.

19. See the two articles that close Koyré's *Études d'histoire de la pensée philosophique:* "Les Philosophes et la machine" and "Du monde de l'à-peu-près à l'univers de la précision" (Paris: Gallimard, 1971). The two texts had been originally published in *Critique* in 1948.

20. Whence the preeminent status given to astronomy, optics, and harmony. See Simon, 1988, 182–83. Following E. Garin (*Moyen Age et Renaissance* [Paris: Gallimard, 1969]), these disciplines are opposed to scholarly astrology, which claimed to grasp the accidents of the most individual destinies through the configurations of eternal stars and numerical calculations. Whence the scandal astrology caused among certain ancient philosophers, well summarized in Favorinus's works, as reported by Aulus Gellius (*Attic Nights,* vol. 3 [Cambridge, Mass.: Harvard University Press, 1926]), and their insistence on its "foreign" (Chaldean) character.

21. See. H. Scholz, "Die Axiomatik der Alten," an article from 1930 reprinted in *Mathesis Universalis* (Scholz 1961b).

22. It is interesting that H. Scholz, in his *Concise History of Logic* (New York:

Philosophical Library, 1961, 47; the first German edition is from 1931), cites this passage and considers that it is still today what accounts for logic's greatness as a discipline. This is as far away as one can get from logical positivism, and from modern science as well. Recall that Scholz was not only a logician and a philosopher, but also a theologian. More broadly, note how paying attention to mathematical logic can lead certain philosophers to efface the Galilean break: conversely, we know that Koyré had hardly any appreciation for mathematical logic (see "The Liar" [Koyré 1946]).

23. E. Garin (1969, 121–50) goes so far as to affirm that the combination of mathematics and the empirical, which characterizes modern science, was made possible by the return of scholarly astrology, which became accessible again after the twelfth century and flourished in the fifteen and sixteenth centuries. Just as magic, as an action on the world regulated by theorizable principles, gives us the first elements of the modern relation that unites science (as theory and technology) and technology (as the practice and application of science).

24. Moreover, there is an open empirical question: are Koyré's propositions concerning ancient science incontestable? Specialists discuss this even if for the most part serious authors uphold what is essential to his view; see Thomas Kuhn, "Mathematical versus Experimental Traditions in the Development of Physical Science," in *The Essential Tension* (Chicago: University of Chicago Press, 1977), 31–65; and Simon 1988.

25. Such as Archimedes and Lucretius, according to M. Serres in *The Birth of Physics* (London: Clinamen, 2001 [1977]). Independently of Serres's theses, Archimedes is often taken as an example of just such a combination of mathematics and the empirical, one that was not without technological applications. See, among others, G. Lloyd, *Greek Science after Aristotle* (London: Chatto and Windus, 1973), 40–48, 91–95. Moreover, what we know of Archimedes's doctrinal positions confirms that he was himself adept at the fundamental principles of ancient *epistème*. See his incomplete work entitled "The Method of Mechanical Theorems," addressed to Eratosthenes (a fragment is cited in Lloyd 1973, 91–92).

26. This is the question Lacan asks in his seventh seminar. He did not, however, turn this exoteric oral intervention into a writing. This proves that he thought he was unable to bring to completion what was required for knowledge, and a reading of the seminar confirms this. What also confirms this is the lack of any subsequent attempt by him to relate what he advanced in that text about ethics to what, later on, he advances under the heading of *bien dire* (see, for example, *Television*, Lacan 1990). We thus know very little about Lacanian ethics: only that one would, in principle, be possible.

The question of morality in an infinite, mathematized, and precise universe is of course an open one. On this point I refer to G. Lardreau, *La Véracité* (Paris: Verdier, 1993) (see especially the second book, first section—pp. 130–275—and the close examination to which he submits the Lacanian intervention [pp. 159–60 and note 16); and to J. Vuillemin, *L'Intuitionnisme kantien* (Paris: Vrin, 1994). On the general question of ethics in a universe in which mathematics is the science of being and not just the language of science, see Alain Badiou, especially his *Ethics* (London: Verso, 2013 [1993]).

27. [By Francois de la Rochefoucauld, 1613–1680, France, writer and memoirist. – *Trans.*]

28. Copernicus, Freud writes, demonstrated that "our earth was not the centre of the universe but only a tiny fragment of a cosmic system" (Freud 1963 [1917], 285). Lacan, basing himself on Koyré (*The Astronomical Revolution* [New York: Dover, 1992]), takes this presentation to be "mythical"; to his way of thinking, the revolutionary step was accomplished not by Copernicus but by Kepler, and it was not about geocentrism but the substitution of the ellipse for the circle. See "Subversion of the Subject and the Dialectic of Desire," Lacan 2006k, 674–75; "Radiophonie," Lacan 2001e (1970), 422; and *Seminar XX*, Lacan 1998 (1975), 40–43. Whatever the case may be, we find, in Lacan, a concern for historical precision that separates him from historicism—the latter proceeds by broad generalizations.

On the Galilean rejection of the Gestalt, in an entirely different context, see J.-C. Milner, *Introduction à une science du langage* (Paris: Seuil, 1989), 632–33.

If one wants to quibble with Freud's facts, Freud can also be reproached for having cited Wallace alongside Darwin, because Wallace did quite a bit to salvage humanity's self-love. (See, for example, Stephen Jay Gould, "Natural Selection and the Human Brain: Darwin vs. Wallace," in *The Panda's Thumb* [New York: Norton, 1992], 47–58).

29. See *Seminar XVII* (in its entirety), Lacan 2007 (1991); "Radiophonie," Lacan 2001e (1970), 444–47; "Allocution sur l'enseignement," Lacan 2001d (1970), 297–305; *Television*, Lacan 1990a (1973); and *Seminar XX*, Lacan 1998 (1975), 16–17. See also this book, chapter 3, p. 55.

30. On this point, see the works of Kuhn and in particular his collection *The Essential Tension* (Chicago: University of Chicago Press, 1977), which is more explicit on the confrontation with Popper than *The Structure of Scientific Revolutions* is (Chicago: University of Chicago Press, 1996 [1962]).

31. A linking together of letters, the possible universe, and the dice throw can be found in Kripke: see in particular *Naming and Necessity* (Cambridge, Mass.: Harvard University Press, 1980), 16–21. Quite obviously, we are setting aside any horror Kripke might feel at being brought so close to Mallarmé or Lacan, assuming he even knows who they are.

32. In other words, the doctrine of the letter rests on a logic of two times. The reader can confirm that Lacan's formula $S_1 (S_1(S_1(S_1 \rightarrow S_2)))$—found in *Seminar XX*, Lacan 1998 (1975), 143—is just the rendering of this logic into letters.

33. Which infinity is at stake? Ultimately, the infinity which has been rendered into letters: that of the mathematicians, that is to say, Cantor's. But he was a latecomer. At the origin of Galilean science, paradoxically at the very moment when the universe is said to be mathematized and the universe is linked to the infinite, there is no mathematics of infinity. Because of this hysteresis, positive infinity and the negative indefinite oscillated back and forth, which Descartes was the first to signal.

34. See "L'Étourdit," Lacan 2001f (1972), 453: "In order to be the language most suitable for scientific discourse, mathematics must be the science without conscience promised by our good old Rabelais . . . ; the gay science that prides itself on being the ruin of the soul."

35. Walter Benjamin reports the following saying by Leiris (editors have not been able to figure out whether it is Michel Leiris or Pierre Leyris): "the word *'familier'* in Baudelaire is full of mystery and disquiet" (Benjamin 2006, 156). This is not unconnected to Baudelaire's phrase *"n'importe où hors du monde"* ["anywhere out of this world" – *Trans.*], and from the non-familiar as a refuge.

Chapter 3

1. See É. Balibar, *Lieux et noms de la vérité* (Paris: Éditions de L'Aube, 1997).

2. On Althusser, see the collection *Politique et philosophie dans l'oeuvre de Louis Althusser*, ed. S. Lazarus (Paris: Presses Universitaires de France, 1993).

3. Allow me to refer here to my own *Archéologie d'un échec* (Paris: Seuil, 1993).

4. [Foucault's *Discipline and Punish* was first published in the series Bibliothèque des histoires by Gallimard. – *Trans.*]

5. [These are allusions to works by Koyré. – *Trans.*]

6. [This quote is not included in the English translation of Foucault's book. It can be found in Char's *The Brittle Age* (Char 2009, 45). – *Trans.*]

7. Read the somewhat different commentary that P. Veyne develops in *René Char en ses poems* (Paris: Gallimard, 1990), 499. [Milner is alluding to the famous Maoist slogan here, "It is always right to rebel against reactionaries." – *Trans.*]

8. I add that this proof is a good example of apagogic reasoning.

9. This was just one of the issues. Lacan emphasizes it more clearly than anyone else did (see "The Instance of the Letter," Lacan 2006f, 439 note 6). The greatest Russian-language poets in the 1920s (which means in some respects the greatest poets in the world) were convinced that the Revolution called for a new language and that it was their job to construct it. Stalin rejected this. Even before the theorem was formulated explicitly (it dates from 1950), there was already a politics inspired by it. Whence Mayakovsky's despair, which led to his death; whence the strictly ambivalent relations, between protection and ferocity, that Stalin had with poets: they were called upon to change culture without changing language, and to make non-change in language the very means for the change in culture. Stalin knew very well that they would only succeed if they thought that they could change language. Their illusion was thus at once criminal and necessary to their success. They had to be persecuted if they failed, and they had to be persecuted if they succeeded. [Vladimir Mayakovsky, 1893–1930, Soviet poet, playwright, and actor. – *Trans.*]

10. "Only my theory of language as structure of the unconscious can be said to be implied by Marxism, if, that is, you are not more demanding than the material implication with which our most recent logic is satisfied" ("Responses

to Students of Philosophy," Lacan 1990c [1966], 111). Recall that the relation "A materially implies B" is only false if A is true and B is false; it is true in all other cases. In other words, those who held Marxism to be true (at the time they were quite numerous) must hold that Lacan is true; but the falsehood of Marxism does not mean that Lacan is false, and the truth of Lacan does not mean that Marxism is true. Notice that Lacan speaks only of language; remember that, as far as language is concerned, according to Lacan, Marxism boils down to Stalin.

11. [Milner is alluding to the discussions that took place between Kojève and Leo Strauss regarding tyranny. They are included in the revised and extended edition of Strauss's *On Tyranny* (Chicago: University of Chicago Press, 2013), 135–76. –*Trans.*]

12. This explains the proposition from *Seminar XX:* "there is some emergence of psychoanalytic discourse whenever there is a movement from one discourse to another" (Lacan 1998 [1975], 16). Every discursive change is a major break; every break is an interpretation; and every interpretation is part of analytic discourse's framework.

13. But see J.-A. Miller, "Encyclopédie" (Miller 1981), 35–44, a republication of the article "Jacques Lacan" from the *Encyclopedia Universalis*, 1979; see especially 41–42.

14. The archiphoneme /T/ is not distinct from /t/ and /d/. So this means that the singular *Rat* (which contains a /T/) and the plural *Räder* (which contains a /d/) are not distinct as far as the dental occlusive is concerned; this is how we can understand the unity of the word in the singular and the plural.

15. The comparison to Galileo imposes itself on us even more strongly if we go back to "The Assayer," section 48 (Galileo 1960 [1623]), 308–14; see Redondi's commentary as well (Redondi 1989, 56–57). There it appears that the reduction of sensible qualities reduces them to rational properties: figure (limited by an exterior), spatial position (by means of a doctrine of relative space), time (by means of a doctrine of relative time), contact with other bodies, etc. Now, structural linguistics also consists in reducing every property down to a relation: the relation of distinctive opposition. The analogy can be pushed further: any given phonematic system can be considered an inertial system; even if its phonetic materiality were to change, it is taken to be identical to itself if its internal differential relations remain the same (for example, the French phonological system remains the same whether the /r/ is "rolled" or not, because its internal relations are not affected by this variation). The absence of simultaneity between independent inertial systems leads to the view that there are no homophonic phonemes shared among distinct phonematic systems (even when phonetics could attribute identical sensible properties to their supports).

16. See the following propositions, taken from "The Instance of the Letter": (1) language is "what essentially distinguishes human society from natural societies," (2) "they have allowed language to attain the status in experience of a scientific object," and (3) "This is what permits linguistics to present itself in the pilot position in this domain, around which a reclassification of the sciences is signaling . . . a revolution in knowledge" (Lacan 2006f, 414). Proposition (3)

uses the word "revolution," which is associated with Copernicus and more generally with the Galilean break: proposition (1) states that language does not belong
to nature.

17. "The form of mathematization in which the discovery of the *phoneme* is
inscribed" ("The Function and Field of Speech and Language in Psychoanalysis,"
Lacan 2006d, 235).

18. I would like to point out in passing how surprising this line of reasoning is: a conclusion is made about the identity of something solely on the basis
of a dissimilarity among qualities, and a mutual exclusion. This line of reasoning
is only valid if the set of phonematic entities and the totality of contexts are finite. If the totality is infinite (for example, in the case of vocabulary), the line of
reasoning is flimsy. A mythical version of this, strange and disquieting, is found
in the Borges story "The Theologians": two theologians adhere to opposed doctrines and fight without ever encountering each other. One obtains the other's
condemnation, and he dies at the stake. Ultimately it turns out that for God "(the
orthodox and the heretic, the abominator and the abominated, the accuser and
the victim) were a single person" (Borges 2004, 34). The two theologians were,
we could say, like two combinatory variants in complementary distribution. Note
that the theological question in the story is about knowing if time is a closed
set. In a larger sense, the doctrine on identity found here can be put this way: if
two entities can be co-present, we have to conclude that they are distinct; if two
entities are identical, then they are separate; in particular, what is identical to
itself is separate from itself and so does not have a Self to which it can be identical. We find here the seeds of some of the theory of the subject's fundamental
theorems. We can also see here the dramatization portrayed in "Logical Time"
(Lacan 2006c): men recognize each other as men; from this moment on, they
see that they are distinct from each other. In short, identity is real, but separative;
resemblance unites, but is imaginary.

19. We know that this axiom is essential to Cartesianism, in metaphysics as
well as in physics. It is the basis for the affirmation that there cannot be a void. It
is interesting to note that Epicurean physics, in which the analogy of the alphabet
and its combinations of characters is so prevalent, does posit—perhaps for this
reason—the existence of the void.

20. As luck would have it, Lacan was not familiar with the work of Harris, who develops a methodologically pure theory of the linguistic chain more
completely in certain respects than Jakobson does. [Zellig Harris, 1909–1992,
American linguist. Milner is alluding especially to Harris's 1951 work *Methods in
Structural Linguistics* (Chicago: University of Chicago Press). –*Trans.*]

21. Lacan was radically opposed to this, due to his doctrine of the barred
Other. As the signifier of pure difference alone, the signifier of the Other is also
the signifier of the fact that there are signifiers, since there are only signifiers if
there is pure difference. Reciprocally, the concept of the Other has to be intrinsically marked by the constitutive difference that links one signifier to another. This
is the antithesis of the idea of God, who could not without contradiction admit
of such an internal difference.

22. Similarly there is a Same, without opposition, which does not depend

on resemblances among properties. This is exactly the Same that Kripke theorizes in *Naming and Necessity* (Kripke 1980). Lacan has recourse to this Same in his theory of repetition ("the real is that which always comes back to the same place," *Seminar XI*, Lacan 1978 [1973], 49). But structural linguistics does not make use of it, so that is not where Lacan gets it from. Since a reference to Kripke was not available at the time, he left this Same untheorized until the RSI knot.

23. It is possible, but not certain, that Lacan came across Queneau's works on the ternary relationship "X takes Y for Z." See C. Berge, "For a Potential Analysis of Combinatory Literature," in *Oulipo* (Normal, Ill.: Dalkey Archive, 1998), 115–25; and R. Queneau, "The Relation X Takes Y for Z," in *Oulipo*, 153–55. It is true that the dates do not line up, since Queneau's contribution in *Oulipo* is from 1965, whereas Lacan's *logion* is from 1960. But it is worth pursuing the investigation further. That said, the differences are as instructive as the resemblances are. For example, for Queneau it is crucial that X could be identical to either Y or Z; for Lacan it is crucial that the difference between X, Y, and Z (whatever its nature is) remains. For Queneau it is crucial that X, Y, and Z be non-specified variables; for Lacan it is crucial that X and Y be stipulated as signifiers and Z as subject. This explains why in Seminar XVII a writing with stipulated variables will be developed on the basis of the three-term relationship: S1 and S2 for X and Y, barred-S for Z. By a supplementary deduction a fourth term is derived (object a). For more details, see p. 83.

24. "In the test of writing *I am thinking: 'therefore I am'* with quotes around the second clause, it is legible that thought only grounds being by knotting itself in speech where every operation goes right to the essence of language" ("Science and Truth," Lacan 2006m, 734). The use of the verb "to knot itself" [*se nouer*] is what proves that there is a signifying chain with two rings here, of thinking and of being (not without a bit of syntactic forcing: the *subject* of "to knot itself" has a discontinuous antecedent in the conjunction "thought + being," and the "itself" [*se*] is reciprocal instead of reflective). In other words, the *cogito* is integrated into the theory of minimal and unspecified structures. This is also what the rewriting in quotation marks implies.

The *cogito* as reread by Lacan is, strictly speaking, the enunciation "therefore I am": from this enunciation, concentrated into a unitary and second signifier (*sum*), a first signifier is retroactively posited: "I think" (*cogito*); the real subject insists in the movement (from the second to the first, from the first to the second) between these two signifiers. This movement is signaled by the alternating ephemerality of the "therefore" (*ergo*), which is sometimes present and sometimes absent.

This explains why, later on, when every signifying chain is reduced to its minimum (one signifier and another, S1 and S2), the second signifier gets designated as knowledge. This takes us back to the very notion of "I am," which according to commentators is supposed to ground the possibility of knowledge as such, thanks to, let's remember, the passage to a thought with qualities. But S2 is precisely this very passage. The theory of discourse and the doctrine of Seminar XX (sessions 8 and 11) depend on this analysis of the *cogito*.

We note in passing that, presented this way, the *cogito* is an example of private language in Wittgenstein's sense (as the unconscious itself is too, if the unconscious is structured like a language): it is thus vulnerable, like any private language, to the Wittgenstein-Kripke paradox. The paradox can be summarized as follows: what assures us that God the deceiver is not able to change the rules regarding how the lexeme *sum* is used, as well as those for the conclusion-operator *ergo*, between the moment when I begin to say "therefore I" and the moment when I end with "am"? Klossowski's *Diana at Her Bath* (New York: Marsilio, 1990 [1956]) tries to be the Ovidian myth of this eventuality. President Schreber also gives us examples of declarations that are close to "therefore I" (see "On a Question Prior to Any Possible Treatment of Psychosis," Lacan 2006g], 452). An instantaneist interpretation could certainly escape such objections, but not an extreme variant of them: what assures me that the deceiver God did not keep the rules for how the lexeme is used intact, except at the very moment when I declared "therefore I am"?

25. Saint Thomas summarizes this as follows: "*omne ens est unum, verum, bonum*" ["every being is one, true, and good" –*Trans.*]. On this, see H. Scholz, "Einführung in die kantische Philosophie," 1961c, 172.

26. [Milner is alluding here to the events of May '68. –*Trans.*]

Chapter 4

1. Lévi-Strauss perceived this dis-synchrony without locating it precisely, however. See *The Savage Mind* (Lévi-Strauss 1966 [1962], chapter 9: 245–69). Two series of affirmations can be found in that work: (1) there are major breaks, or at least one in any case: the break between the primitive mind and the thinking that characterizes modern science (269); and (2) this break is not of a historical nature; history is incapable of grasping it; moreover, history is in principle unable to grasp any major break (259–60). In 1965 Lacan himself notes how difficult it is to make Lévi-Strauss's doctrine compatible with Koyré's; but he does not reject it; this confirms that historicism has already ceased to be essential, although it is brought to the fore. But it also confirms that the overall arrangement of the doctrine is not homogeneous; see "Science and Truth," Lacan 2006m, 731.

2. [After Nicolas Bourbaki, the name used by a collective of mathematicians, mostly French, formed in the late 1930s. –*Trans.*]

3. We see that a true professor, eternally replaceable, is the contrary of the true master, who is never able to be replaced. The fact that in contemporary language we so often use the word "master" (think of the very honorable and very honored "*formation des maîtres*" [teacher training/credential programs]) to designate what is the most replaceable thing in the world is just another example of the antithetical meaning of primordial words.

4. The terms are: S1, S2, $, a (see note 10 below); the places are: agent, truth, other, production. An exercise for the reader: using the theory of four discourses, resolve the equivocation that allows for a homonymy between political masters and masters of wisdom. Here's a hint: the issue of pedagogy plays a role in this equivocation.

Notice the timeline. The theory of four discourses is presented in 1970 in *The Other Side of Psychoanalysis* (*Seminar XVII,* Lacan 2007 [1991]); it just barely precedes the doctrine of the matheme (1972) and, to a certain extent, makes it possible.

5. [Jean Laplanche, 1924–2012, French psychoanalyst and student of Lacan's who broke with him in the 1960s; editor of a new translation of Freud's complete works starting in 1983. – *Trans.*]

6. [In English in the original. – *Trans.*]

7. We suspect that the doctrine of the matheme intersects in a dramatic fashion with the question of the position of the analyst. Will it be said in fact that the latter does not intervene as a subject? But if he does intervene as a subject, can we deny that he is irreplaceable? And if he is not able to be replaced, is he not structurally in a different position than the one he has in the configuration of modern science? More precisely still, is he not in the same position as the Masters of wisdom? (This is what is compelling about the idea of a Lacan-Gurdjieff.) [George Gurdjieff, 1866 or 1877 to 1949, Armenian/Greek mystic. – *Trans.*] But if the analyst is a Master, then there is no matheme for psychoanalysis, psychoanalysis does not belong to the modern universe, and Freud did not exist. An essential part of the Lacanian program consists in resolving this antinomy.

8. [In French "*senti-maître*" would also resonate with the unit of measure, the centimeter. – *Trans.*]

9. In other words, Chomskian transformational operations involve letters, not signifiers. Reciprocally, the theory of four discourses, which is literal, depends in fact on a transformational technique. This goes together with the fact that its terms are qualified and not unspecified. The fact that each literal transformation is registered, in historical representations, as a catastrophe (what Lacan calls a "shift") is due to historical representations.

10. The quartet is introduced in *Seminar XVII,* Lacan 2007 (1991). In Seminar XX it is reduced to an even more minimal form, only S1 and S2 (see *Seminar XX,* Lacan 1998 [1975]; and above, chapter 2, note 33). We can consider these writings to be the mathemes of the signifier. To be completely exact, these mathemes are of the order of letters; they thus capture signifiers in letters. How they do this can be made more precise: signifiers as such are not qualified, but in the mathemes S1 and S2 they are qualified: S1 is the Master and S2 is knowledge. Once they are qualified, we are in the domain of letters, not signifiers. On S2 as knowledge, see above, chapter 3, note 24.

11. See "L'Étourdit," Lacan 2001f (1972), 458, 465, and passim. An additional explanation: sexuality is essentially nothing other than the radical principle of a move the speaking being always makes: to include itself in the ranks of a whole, or outside of them, on the basis of some property Φ: the sexual writings are thus an exercise in collective logic; see above, chapter 2, p. 45. The first line, that of the Whole, confirming itself by the constructability of what limits it, goes by the name Man; the definite article, which in French is also a totalizing article, is thus permissible for it: Man exists [*l'Homme existe*]. The second line, that of the not-all, of the impermissibility of the whole when there is nothing that marks a limit, goes by the name Woman; the definite article is not permissible for it: the

Woman does not exist. What is the relationship between these names and what everyone calls men and women?

In structural phonology, certain purely combinatory properties were called "unvoiced" (or "occlusive" or "nasal," etc.) and other properties, also combinatory, were called "voiced" ("non-occlusive," "non-nasal," etc.). These phonological names are homonyms of phonetic names, describing substantial phonic properties that can be observed by experimental phoneticians. Phonologists, using these homonymical names, affirmed three things: (1) that phonology is not phonetics; that the term "unvoiced" in phonology is about structural properties and in itself says nothing about these phonic properties; that the phonological being called "unvoiced" is thus not necessarily unvoiced from the point of view of phonetic substance; but (2) it just so happens that the phonological name "unvoiced" and the phonetic name "unvoiced" coincide, and (3) this happens more often than not.

Likewise, the position called Man (or Woman) is structural and says nothing about the male (or female) somatic qualities of the subject who occupies it. But it may be the case that these properties coincide with the position called Man (or Woman) and the subject's male (or female) somatic properties. The hypothesis (which is refutable) is that that this happens more often than not.

12. Thus the sexual writings can foresee and explain why, among the common people, woman is called *la bourgeoise* ("L'Étourdit," Lacan 2001f [1972], 469). It is possible and legitimate to pursue exercises like this: to note, for example, that the English word "queen" (the Indo-European name for woman, analogous to the Greek *gynè*) designates at one and the same time the queen and the prostitute (today more specifically an effeminate male prostitute); that Jean Genet gives the name Divine to a queer person, and that Divine says of herself "I am the Quite-Quite" [*Toute-Toute:* see Genet 1961 (1953), 111. –*Trans.*]; that the guillotine is called the Widow [*la Veuve*] and masturbation is called *Veuve Poignet* [literally Widow Wrist]; all of this is empirically significant, despite its minuteness; the matheme proves itself to be able to calculate it. For the four discourses, the comparable procedures are with the oeuvre: see *Seminar XVII*, Lacan 2007 (1991). This matrix-like character is in line with Freud ("I, a man, love a man," "a child is being beaten," etc.). But Freud only had grammar at his disposal for his calculus. In the wake of the matheme, grammar turns out to be only alluding to its true principle: literal calculus. To mathematize more overtly than Freud ever did is thus to make a more decisive return to Freud than the one that took place in the first classicism.

13. [*"Litterâ scire licet"* means "it is permitted to know thanks to the letter" or "one can know thanks to the letter." The title of the École de la Cause Freudienne's journal, *Scilicet*, echoes this Latin phrase. –*Trans.*]

14. Lacan's own doctrine of intuition seems to contradict Brouwer's. Inasmuch as the latter can be understood at all, it is a doctrine about the fullness of the intuiting subject (which eventually authorizes all sorts of deviations, including those of Guénon or Evola; Brouwer seems to have let himself go to the worst). According to Lacan, the instant of intuition is an instant when the subject is

voided out—which can be read in the very word "evidence." [L. E. J. Brouwer, 1881–1966, Dutch mathematician and philosopher. René Guénon, 1886–1954, French author and esoteric thinker who converted to Islam and called for an infusion of Eastern ideas into Western thinking. Julius Evola, 1898–1974, Italian pan-European fascist intellectual. –*Trans.*]

15. See the totality of Alain Badiou's work, but especially *Being and Event* (2006 [1988], London: Continuum), 247–51. Notice the radical difference between Lacan and Badiou; the second refers to a mathematics endowed with the procedures of deduction and capable of apagogical reasoning. In his most recent works, Badiou tends to accentuate the difference and not to minimize it.

16. [See chapter 2, note 14 for the use of "literalizing" here. –*Trans.*]

17. "Man thus speaks, but it is because the symbol has made him man" (Lacan 2006d, 229). It could be said that the concept of the symbol consists precisely of its inability to distinguish between letters and signifiers. This is exactly the status it has in Saussure (in a fragment apparently prior to the courses on general linguistics, cited by Starobinski in *Words upon Words: The Anagrams of Ferdinand de Saussure* [New Haven, Conn.: Yale University Press, 1979], 5–6): the properties of the signifier are conferred upon the rune, an entity of letters. The impasse of the anagrams project is due to this lack of a distinction.

18. For a classic account of mathematical logic as a calculus of letters, see P. Rosenbloom, *The Elements of Mathematical Logic* (New York: Dover, 1950), II–III and 152–80.

19. Reciprocally, if the mathematicity of mathematics is not defined by letters, then, by a cascade of consequences, the Galilean break is erased. One illustrious example of this view, among others, and infinitely admirable, is A. Lautman. [A. Lautman, 1908–1944, France, philosopher of mathematics, member of the Resistance who was shot by the Germans as an escaped prisoner of war. –*Trans.*] According to Lautman, mathematicity is the contemplation of objective mathematical beings (independent of the letters that happen to designate them); consequently, the fact that a mathematical physics is possible means that the *Timaeus* needs to be rewritten. Modern science can and must adapt itself to Platonic *epistèmè*. See, for its clarity, the debate between Cavaillès and Lautman, reproduced in Cavaillès, *Oeuvres complètes de philosophie des sciences* (Paris: Hermann, 1994), 593–630, and especially 605–9. [Jean Cavaillès, 1903–1944, France, philosopher of mathematics, member of the Resistance, shot by the Gestapo. –*Trans.*]

There is a similar result if the logic-ness of logic is not defined in terms of letters; see above, chapter 2, note 22.

20. See the second session, entitled "To Jakobson," in which "L'Étourdit" is explicitly referred to. Its central theme is the "change of discourse." See equally, in a protreptic mode, the session of April 19, 1977, entitled "Vers un signifiant nouveau" (Lacan 1979, 16).

21. [The translation is modified. –*Trans.*]

22. Lemma one: the expression "subject of the unconscious" is infelicitous; it is only legitimate because it is easy to use: it stands for the real coincidence

between subject and individual. I leave it to the learned whether the Cartesian doctrine on the union of the soul and body has to be evoked here. Lemma two: since the individual concerned is the biological individual (see Lacan 2006m, 743), the unconscious with which he is affected is biological as well. Lacan's hypothesis also says: the unconscious as a biological entity coincides, link by link, with signifying chains.

23. [Ernst Jünger, 1895–1998, German memoirist and writer. His *The Worker* (Evanston, Ill.: Northwestern University Press, 2017), originally published in 1932, is influenced by Nietzsche and is critical of Marx. *– Trans.*]

24. [This sentence rephrases one of Pascal's *Pensées*, no. 887 (London: Penguin), 275. *– Trans.*]

25. I will permit myself to refer to my own *Les Noms indistincts* (Paris: Le Seuil, 1983). Notice that the theory of the triliteral knot is not a theory of the unspecified. It is even its complete contrary. In order to be fruitful, it is not sufficient that a Borromean property be isolated, although this is necessary to its definition; in addition, each loop must be qualified; the letters, R, S, I, stand for these qualities. If the loops are qualified, they are not unspecified. The triliteral knot intervenes at the antipodes of unspecified structure, which does not qualify anything. For this very reason, the former can found and legitimize the latter, as a regional theory.

26. *Les Noms indistincts* adheres to this view (Milner 1983).

27. Such is the kernel of sense in the article "La Psychiatrie anglaise et la guerre" (Lacan 2001a); we can find in it, beyond the praise given to England, the description of an adversary to come: the WASP world, subordinating England to the United States and reuniting in each of the two countries, in the name of the ideal science, what is most inimical to free thinking. The IPA is a version of this world. In 1960 Lacan wrote of "the notorious deviations . . . in England and in America" ("The Subversion of the Subject," Lacan 2006k, 672); the reference to England here prohibits us from seeing this as a variant of his denunciation of the *American way of life*.

28. This text, read out loud at the seminar of March 15, 1980, is a response to Althusser, who is given the name "Monsieur A., philosopher." However, Lacan is also calling attention to the title of a work by Tristan Tzara: *Monsieur Aa, the Antiphilosopher*. Notice the statement "philosophy is a thing of the finite"; it is not illegitimate to interpret it in the following way: "philosophy has no place in the infinite universe." I thank F. Regnault for calling my attention to this reference.

29. Lacan here refers to the *Essay on Indifference* by Lamennais (London: John McQueen, 1895 [1817]). [Hugues-Felicité Robert de Lamennais, 1782–1854, French Catholic priest and philosopher during the Restoration. *– Trans.*] The reference is found again in *Seminar XI*, Lacan 1978 (1973), 264. Notice that the Freudian indifference to politics has limits that one does not have to agree with: a marked bias in favor of the English political system is not ruled out. Although this prejudice has been almost mandatory in European letters since the eighteenth century, it is not without some naïveté, and it contains the seeds of some later developments. See above, note 27.

Chapter 5

1. [See "Letter of Dissolution," Lacan 1990d. – *Trans.*]

2. Of course, the historical problems are much more complicated. In particular, keep in mind that Descartes was loath to use the concept of infinity when it came to the universe.

3. Notice the emergence of the word *pathème* in Seminar R. S. I., two years after *Encore* and "L'Étourdit" ("R. S. I. séminaire du 11 mars 1975: Le Pathème du phallus," Lacan 1975d). One does not have to be a great genius to hear a foreclusive *pas* in it, one that affects the matheme just as it affects the operator "all" in the doctrine of sexuation (this is not to rule out other connections: with *pathein*, for example).

4. The idea emerged in 1968. According to one of its authors (in a personal communication), it was premature at the time, but also premonitory. Five years later, it had become true.

5. The developments in the session of April 19, 1977, entitled "Vers une signifiant nouveau" (Lacan 1979, 15–16), are quite revealing; basing himself on the works of F. Cheng on Chinese written poetry, and renewing his homage to Jakobson, Lacan addresses himself to psychoanalysts: "to eventually be inspired by something like poetry in order to intervene as a psychoanalyst? This is in fact what I want to turn you toward. . . . It is not necessary to take our speech to be on the side of articulated logic—although I slide into that on occasion." It is difficult not to take what is being said of logic here as a dismissal of the matheme.

6. [Milner is alluding here and in the next few paragraphs to Mallarmé's poem "A Throw of the Dice" (Mallarmé 1994). Its complete title is "A Throw of the Dice Will Never Abolish Chance." Earlier references by Milner to dice throws and contingency are alluding to this poem as well. – *Trans.*]

7. [Milner is alluding to a passage in André Breton's *Mad Love*: "Convulsive beauty will be veiled-erotic, fixed-explosive, magic-circumstantial, or it will not be" (Breton 1987 [1937], 19). – *Trans.*]

8. [Constellations getting "cold from forgetfulness" is a line from Mallarmé's "A Throw of the Dice" (Mallarmé 1994). – *Trans.*]

9. On Lacan's relation to Wittgenstein, see É. Roudinesco, *Jacques Lacan and Co.* (Chicago: University of Chicago Press, 1990), 561–64; and her *Jacques Lacan* (New York: Columbia University Press, 1997), 345–46.

10. [Milner is referring to the poet Rimbaud, who lived and worked in Ethiopia for a while after he stopped writing poetry. – *Trans.*]

11. It is worth giving the quote by Fontenelle in its entirety: "I would have my hand full of truths that I would not open up for the people." This at least is how O. Guerlac gives it in *Les Citations francaises* (Paris: A. Colin, 1954). We see the classical political doctrine of the letter here, which moderns, as such, had renounced since the Enlightenment and the Revolution (see Leo Strauss). Notice that Lacan has purified the citation and depoliticized it; this is because he is modern (especially because of science's Core Doctrine). He can hesitate between opening and closing his hand; but at any rate this is not in order to exclude the

people [*le peuple*]. At most, the rabble (*Television*, Lacan 1990a [1973], 43), but they are not the same thing.

12. [*The Indiscreet Jewels* or *The Talking Jewels*, a novel by Denis Diderot (1713–1784), published anonymously in 1718, in which a magic ring makes women's genitals (the jewels in question) speak. – *Trans.*]

13. Let's recall that the ethic of *bien dire* is proposed by Lacan in response to the Kantian question "What must I do?" (*Was soll ich tun?*) (*Television*, Lacan 1990a [1973], 41). In Wittgenstein, the *sollen* bears on what cannot be said, thus one does not say it, one shows it (*Tractatus*, 6.421 [Wittgenstein 1998, 108]). In Lacan, the *sollen* bears on what cannot be said entirely; thus one must say it well.

14. Kripke's skeptical interpretation of Wittgenstein has been rejected by competent authors. And the interpretation of ancient skepticism, made classic by Brochard especially, has been contested, with solid arguments, by J.-P. Dumont. But this hardly matters here. There is a way that Lacan characterizes skepticism: "it is holding the subjective position that *one can know nothing*" (*Seminar XI*, Lacan 1978 [1973], 223). He took skepticism to be both heroic and unimaginable to moderns, especially because of Descartes and the *cogito*. But what remains of the *cogito* at the time of the knot and *lalangue*?

15. [Milner is alluding to the opening lines of Lucretius's poem *De rerum natura* [*On the Nature of Things*], which constitute a hymn to the goddess Venus. – *Trans.*]

Afterword to the English Translation

1. Jean-Claude Milner, *Introduction à une science du langage* (Paris: Le Seuil, 1989).

2. This book was published by Seuil in 1978 in its series Connexions du champ freudien. An English translation by Ann Banfield was published under the title *For the Love of Language* (New York: St. Martin's Press, 1990).

3. This communication was published in number 25 of the review *Ornicar?* in October 1982. It forms the first chapter of my book *Les Noms indistincts*, published by Seuil in 1983, and is also in the series Connexions du champ freudien. The bulk of the work comes from a course given at the Department of Psychoanalysis of University Paris-VIII in 1980.

4. Ernst Mach, *Die Mechanik in inhrer Entwickelung historisch-kristisch dargestellt* (Leipzig, 1883). The work had a global impact. An English translation was published as early as 1893 under the title *The Science of Mechanics*. The French translation was titled *La Mécanique: Exposé historique et critique de son development* (Paris: Librarie Scientifique A. Hermann, 1904; republished by Éditions J. Gabay, 1987).

5. Éric Laurent, *L'Envers de la biopolitique* (Paris: Navarin/Le Champ Freudien, 2016).

6. Jacques Lacan, "La Troisième," *La Cause Freudienne*, no. 79 (2011): 11–33. The text was delivered in 1975 and published for the first time in that same

year in the *Lettres de l'École Freudienne*. It has just been translated into English under the title "The Third" in *The Lacanian Review* 7 (Spring 2019): 83–109.

7. See Jean-Claude Milner, "Back and Forth from Letter to Homophony," *Problemi International* 1, no. 1 (2017): 81–98.

8. Roman Jakobson, "Une Microscopie du dernier 'Spleen' dans *Les Fleurs du mal*," in *Questions de poétique* (Paris: Le Seuil, 1973), 420–35; first published in *Tel Quel* 29 (1967): 12–24.

9. See above, p. 106.

10. See above, p. 107.

11. *Television*, Lacan 1990a (1973), 46.

12. R. Jakobson, "Why 'Mama' and 'Papa'?" in *Perspectives in Psychological Theory*, ed. B. Kaplan and S. Wapner (New York: International Universities Press, 1960), 123–34.

13. "Seminar on 'The Purloined Letter,'" Lacan 2006a, 10.

14. David Hayman, *Joyce et Mallarmé: Les Élements mallarméens dans l'oeuvre de Joyce* (Paris: Lettres Modernes, 1956). Many Anglophone Joyce specialists seem to be unaware of this work.

15. "Joyce le symptôme," Lacan 2001i: for the history of this text, which begins in 1975, see the bibliographical note in *Autres écrits* on p. 610.

16. I refer to Éric Laurent's commentary in *L'Envers de la biopolitique*, 65 (and to other passages in the same work, signaled by the author in note 65 of page 65); as well as to Jacques-Alain Miller, "L'Inconscient et le corps parlant," *La Cause du Désir* 88 (November 2014): 104–14.

17. Sigmund Freud, "On the Universal Tendency toward Debasement in the Sphere of Love" (Freud 1957 [1912]), 189.

18. "The Third," Lacan 2019 (1975), 94.

19. Jean-Claude Milner, "Lacan's Later Work and the *Declaration of the Rights of Man*," *The Lacanian Review*, no. 7 (Spring 2019): 202–8.

Bibliography

Badiou, Alain. 2006 (1988). *Being and Event*. Translated by Oliver Feltham. London: Continuum.

———. 2013 (1993). *Ethics: An Essay on the Understanding of Evil*. Translated by Peter Hallward. London: Verso.

Balibar, Étienne. 1997. *Lieux et noms de la vérité*. Paris: Éditions de l'Aube.

———. 2017. "'*Ego sum, ego existo*': Descartes on the Verge of Heresy." In *Citizen Subject: Foundations for Philosophical Anthropology*, 55–73. Translated by Steven Miller, foreword by Emily Apter. New York: Fordham University Press.

Benjamin, Walter. 2006. *The Writer of Modern Life: Essays on Charles Baudelaire*. Edited by Michael W. Jennings, translated by Howard Eiland, Edmund Jephcott, Rodney Livingston, and Harry Zohn. Cambridge, Mass.: Belknap.

Benveniste, Émile. 1955. "Homophonies radicales en indo-européen." *Bulletin de la Société de Linguistique de Paris*, vol. 51 (1955): 14–41.

Berge, Claude. 1986. "For a Potential Analysis of Combinatory Literature." In *Oulipo: A Primer of Potential Literature*, translated and edited by Warren F. Motte, Jr., 115–25. Normal, Ill.: Dalkey Archive.

Beyssade, Jean-Marie. 1979. *La Philosophie première de Descartes: Le Temps et la cohérence de la métaphysique*. Paris: Flammarion.

Bidez, J. 1943. *Un singulier naufrage littéraire dans l'antiquité: A la recherche des épaves de l'Aristote perdu*. Brussels: Collection Lebègue.

Borges, Jorge-Luis. 2004. "The Theologians." In *The Aleph and Other Stories*, translated by Andrew Hurley, 26–34. London: Penguin.

Bourbaki, Nicolas. 1968. *Elements of Mathematics: Theory of Sets*. Reading, Mass.: Addison-Wesley.

Breton, André. 1987 (1937). *Mad Love*. Translated by Mary Ann Caws. Lincoln: University of Nebraska Press.

Cahiers pour l'Analyse, vol. 9 (Summer 1968). http://cahiers.kingston.ac.uk/vol09/.

Cavaillès, Jean. 1994. *Oeuvres completes de philosophie des sciences*. Paris: Hermann.

Char, René. 2009. *The Brittle Age and Returning Upland*. Translated by Gustaf Sobin, foreword by Mary Ann Caws. Denver, Colo.: Counterpath.

Descartes, René. 1998. (1637, 1641). *Discourse on Method and Meditations on First Philosophy*. Translated by Donald A. Cress. Indianapolis, Ind.: Hackett.

Detienne, Marcel. 1999 (1967). *The Masters of Truth in Archaic Greece*. Translated by Janet Lloyd, foreword by Pierre Vidal-Naquet. Cambridge, Mass.: Zone.

Foucault, Michel. 1973 (1966). *The Order of Things: An Archaeology of the Human Sciences.* New York: Vintage.

Freud, Sigmund. 1953a (1900). *The Standard Edition of the Complete Psychological Works of Sigmund Freud. Volume IV: The Interpretation of Dreams (First Part).* Edited and translated by James Strachey, in collaboration with Anna Freud, assisted by Alix Strachey and Alan Tyson. London: Hogarth.

———. 1953b (1900). *The Standard Edition of the Complete Psychological Works of Sigmund Freud. Volume V: The Interpretation of Dreams (Second Part) and On Dreams.* Edited and translated by James Strachey, in collaboration with Anna Freud, assisted by Alix Strachey and Alan Tyson. London: Hogarth.

———. 1957 (1912). "On the Universal Tendency to Debasement in the Sphere of Love." In *The Standard Edition of the Complete Psychological Works of Sigmund Freud. Volume XI: Five Lectures on Psychoanalysis, Leonardo da Vinci, and Other Works,* edited and translated by James Strachey, in collaboration with Anna Freud, assisted by Alix Strachey and Alan Tyson, 179–90. London: Hogarth.

———. 1963 (1917). *The Standard Edition of the Complete Psychological Works of Sigmund Freud. Volume XVI (1916–1917): Introductory Lectures on Psycho-Analysis (Part III),* edited and translated by James Strachey, in collaboration with Anna Freud, assisted by Alix Strachey and Alan Tyson. London: Hogarth.

———. 1964 (1925). "On Negation." In *The Standard Edition of the Complete Psychological Works of Sigmund Freud. Volume XIX (1923–1925): The Ego and the Id and Other Works,* edited and translated by James Strachey, in collaboration with Anna Freud, assisted by Alix Strachey and Alan Tyson, 235–239. London: Hogarth.

Galilei, Galileo. 1960 [1623]. "The Assayer." In *The Controversy on the Comets of 1619,* translated by Stillman Drake and C. D. O'Malley, 151–336. Philadelphia: University of Pennsylvania Press.

Garin, Eugenio. 1969. *Moyen Age et Renaissance.* Paris: Gallimard.

Gellius, Aulus. 1926. *Attic Nights, Volume III, Books 14–20.* Loeb Classical Library no. 212. Cambridge, Mass.: Harvard University Press.

Genet, Jean. 1963 (1951). *Our Lady of the Flowers.* Translated by Bernard Frechtman, introduction by Jean-Paul Sartre. New York: Grove.

Gould, Stephen Jay. 1992 (1980). *The Panda's Thumb: More Reflections in Natural History.* New York: Norton.

Gramsci, Antonio. 1971 (1929–35). *Selections from the Prison Notebooks.* Edited and translated by Quintin Hoare and Geoffrey Nowell Smith. New York: International.

Guerlac, Othon. 1954. *Les Citations francaises.* Paris: A. Colin.

Gueroult, Martial. 1984 (1953). *Descartes's Philosophy Interpreted according to the Order of Reasons.* Minneapolis: University of Minnesota Press.

Hallyn, Fernand. 1994. *Le Sens des formes: Études sur la renaissance.* Geneva: Droz.

Harris, Zellig. 1951. *Methods in Structural Linguistics.* Chicago: University of Chicago Press.

Hayman, David. 1956. *Joyce et Mallarmé: Les Élements mallarméens dans l'oeuvre de Joyce*. Paris: Lettres Modernes.

Helmholtz, Hermann von. 1884 (1855). "Über das Sehen des Menschen." In *Vorträge und Reden*, vol. 1: 365–96. Braunschweig: Vieweg und Sohn.

Jaeger, Werner. 1955 (1934). *Aristotle: Fundamentals of the History of His Development*. Translated by Richard Robinson. Oxford: Clarendon.

Jakobson, Roman. 1960. "Why 'Mama' and 'Papa'?" In *Perspectives in Psychological Theory*, edited by B. Kaplan and S. Wapner, 123–34. New York: International Universities Press.

———. 1973. "Une Microscopie du dernier 'Spleen' dans *Les Fleurs du mal*." In *Questions de poétique*, 420–35. Paris: Le Seuil.

Jones, Ernest. 1955. *Life and Work of Sigmund Freud*, vol. 2. London: Hogarth.

Jünger, Ernst. 2017 (1932). *The Worker: Dominion and Form*. Translated by Laurence Paul Hemming and Bogden Costea. Evanston, Ill.: Northwestern University Press.

Klossowski, Pierre. 1990 (1956). *Diana at Her Bath: The Women of Rome*. Translated by Stephen Sartarelli. New York: Eridano's Library.

Kojève, Alexandre. 1964. "L'Origine chrétienne de la science modern." In *Mélanges Alexandre Koyré: L'Aventure de l'esprit*, vol. 2: 295–306. Paris: Hermann.

Koyré, Alexandre. 1946. "The Liar." *Philosophy and Phenomenological Research* 6, no. 3: 344–62.

———. 1965. *Newtonian Studies*. Cambridge, Mass.: Harvard University Press.

———. 1971. *Études d'histoire de la pensée philosophique*. Paris: Gallimard.

———. 1977 (1939). *Galileo Studies*. Translated by John Mepham. New Jersey: Humanities.

———. 1992 (1961). *The Astronomical Revolution: Copernicus, Kepler, Borelli*. Translated by R. E. W. Maddison. New York: Dover.

Kripke, Saul. 1980. *Naming and Necessity*. Cambridge, Mass.: Harvard University Press.

Kuhn, Thomas S. 1977. "Mathematical versus Experimental Traditions in the Development of Physical Science." In *The Essential Tension: Selected Studies in Scientific Tradition and Change*. Chicago: University of Chicago Press.

———. 1996 (1962). *The Structure of Scientific Revolutions*. Chicago: University of Chicago Press.

Lacan, Jacques. 1975a. "Séminaire du 19 decembre 1974." *Ornicar?* 2 (March): 90–97.

———. 1975b. "A la lecture du 17 decembre 1974." *Ornicar?* 2 (March): 98–105.

———. 1975c. "Le Séminaire de Jacques Lacan: Séminaire du 14 janvier 1975." *Ornicar?* 3 (May): 97–103.

———. 1975d. "R. S. I. séminaire du 11 mars 1975: Le Pathème du phallus." *Ornicar?* 5 (Winter): 17–28.

———. 1978 (1973). *The Seminar of Jacques Lacan, Book XI: The Four Fundamental Concepts of Psychoanalysis*. Edited by Jacques-Alain Miller, translated by Alan Sheridan. New York: Norton.

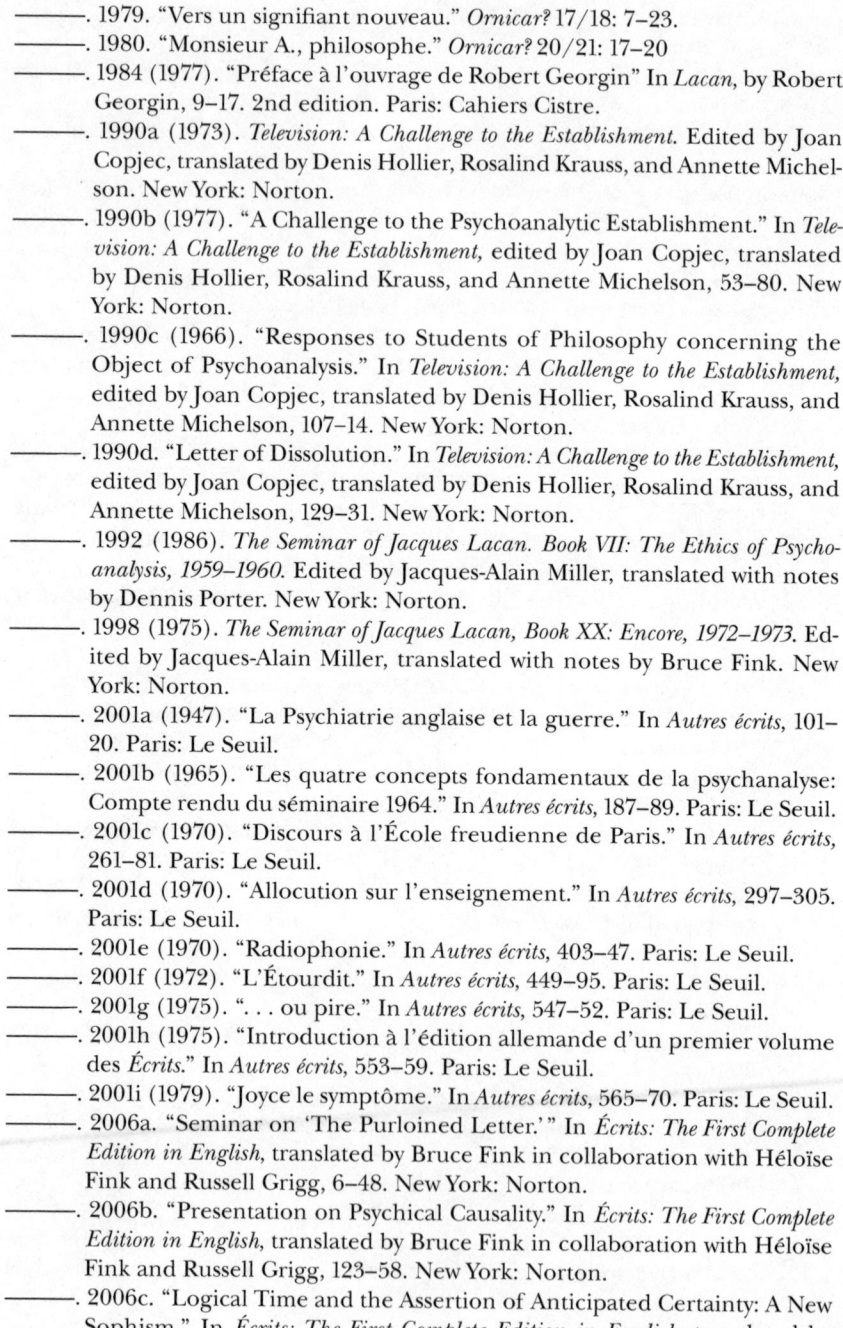

———. 1979. "Vers un signifiant nouveau." *Ornicar?* 17/18: 7–23.

———. 1980. "Monsieur A., philosophe." *Ornicar?* 20/21: 17–20

———. 1984 (1977). "Préface à l'ouvrage de Robert Georgin" In *Lacan*, by Robert Georgin, 9–17. 2nd edition. Paris: Cahiers Cistre.

———. 1990a (1973). *Television: A Challenge to the Establishment.* Edited by Joan Copjec, translated by Denis Hollier, Rosalind Krauss, and Annette Michelson. New York: Norton.

———. 1990b (1977). "A Challenge to the Psychoanalytic Establishment." In *Television: A Challenge to the Establishment,* edited by Joan Copjec, translated by Denis Hollier, Rosalind Krauss, and Annette Michelson, 53–80. New York: Norton.

———. 1990c (1966). "Responses to Students of Philosophy concerning the Object of Psychoanalysis." In *Television: A Challenge to the Establishment,* edited by Joan Copjec, translated by Denis Hollier, Rosalind Krauss, and Annette Michelson, 107–14. New York: Norton.

———. 1990d. "Letter of Dissolution." In *Television: A Challenge to the Establishment,* edited by Joan Copjec, translated by Denis Hollier, Rosalind Krauss, and Annette Michelson, 129–31. New York: Norton.

———. 1992 (1986). *The Seminar of Jacques Lacan. Book VII: The Ethics of Psychoanalysis, 1959–1960.* Edited by Jacques-Alain Miller, translated with notes by Dennis Porter. New York: Norton.

———. 1998 (1975). *The Seminar of Jacques Lacan, Book XX: Encore, 1972–1973.* Edited by Jacques-Alain Miller, translated with notes by Bruce Fink. New York: Norton.

———. 2001a (1947). "La Psychiatrie anglaise et la guerre." In *Autres écrits,* 101–20. Paris: Le Seuil.

———. 2001b (1965). "Les quatre concepts fondamentaux de la psychanalyse: Compte rendu du séminaire 1964." In *Autres écrits,* 187–89. Paris: Le Seuil.

———. 2001c (1970). "Discours à l'École freudienne de Paris." In *Autres écrits,* 261–81. Paris: Le Seuil.

———. 2001d (1970). "Allocution sur l'enseignement." In *Autres écrits,* 297–305. Paris: Le Seuil.

———. 2001e (1970). "Radiophonie." In *Autres écrits,* 403–47. Paris: Le Seuil.

———. 2001f (1972). "L'Étourdit." In *Autres écrits,* 449–95. Paris: Le Seuil.

———. 2001g (1975). ". . . ou pire." In *Autres écrits,* 547–52. Paris: Le Seuil.

———. 2001h (1975). "Introduction à l'édition allemande d'un premier volume des *Écrits.*" In *Autres écrits,* 553–59. Paris: Le Seuil.

———. 2001i (1979). "Joyce le symptôme." In *Autres écrits,* 565–70. Paris: Le Seuil.

———. 2006a. "Seminar on 'The Purloined Letter.'" In *Écrits: The First Complete Edition in English,* translated by Bruce Fink in collaboration with Héloïse Fink and Russell Grigg, 6–48. New York: Norton.

———. 2006b. "Presentation on Psychical Causality." In *Écrits: The First Complete Edition in English,* translated by Bruce Fink in collaboration with Héloïse Fink and Russell Grigg, 123–58. New York: Norton.

———. 2006c. "Logical Time and the Assertion of Anticipated Certainty: A New Sophism." In *Écrits: The First Complete Edition in English,* translated by

Bruce Fink in collaboration with Héloïse Fink and Russell Grigg, 161–75. New York: Norton.

———. 2006d. "The Function and Field of Speech and Language in Psychoanalysis." In *Écrits: The First Complete Edition in English*, translated by Bruce Fink in collaboration with Héloïse Fink and Russell Grigg, 197–268. New York: Norton.

———. 2006e. "The Freudian Thing; or, the Meaning of the Return to Freud in Psychoanalysis." In *Écrits: The First Complete Edition in English*, translated by Bruce Fink in collaboration with Héloïse Fink and Russell Grigg, 334–63. New York: Norton.

———. 2006f. "The Instance of the Letter in the Unconscious; or, Reason since Freud." In *Écrits: The First Complete Edition in English*, translated by Bruce Fink in collaboration with Héloïse Fink and Russell Grigg, 412–41. New York: Norton.

———. 2006g. "On a Question Prior to Any Possible Treatment of Psychosis." In *Écrits: The First Complete Edition in English*, translated by Bruce Fink in collaboration with Héloïse Fink and Russell Grigg, 445–88. New York: Norton.

———. 2006h. "Remarks on Daniel Lagache's Presentation: 'Psychoanalysis and Personality Structure.'" In *Écrits: The First Complete Edition in English*, translated by Bruce Fink in collaboration with Héloïse Fink and Russell Grigg, 543–74. New York: Norton.

———. 2006i. "The Signification of the Phallus." In *Écrits: The First Complete Edition in English*, translated by Bruce Fink in collaboration with Héloïse Fink and Russell Grigg, 575–84. New York: Norton.

———. 2006j. "Kant with Sade." In *Écrits: The First Complete Edition in English*, translated by Bruce Fink in collaboration with Héloïse Fink and Russell Grigg, 645–68. New York: Norton.

———. 2006k. "The Subversion of the Subject and the Dialectic of Desire in the Freudian Unconscious." In *Écrits: The First Complete Edition in English*, translated by Bruce Fink in collaboration with Héloïse Fink and Russell Grigg, 671–702. New York: Norton.

———. 2006m. "Science and Truth." In *Écrits: The First Complete Edition in English*, translated by Bruce Fink in collaboration with Héloïse Fink and Russell Grigg, 726–45. New York: Norton.

———. 2007 (1991). *The Seminar of Jacques Lacan. Book XVII: The Other Side of Psychoanalysis.* Edited by Jacques-Alain Miller, translated by Russell Grigg. New York: Norton.

———. 2011 (1975). "La Troisième." *La Cause Freudienne* 79: 11–33.

———. 2016 (2005). *The Seminar of Jacques Lacan. Book XXIII: The Sinthome.* Edited by Jacques-Alain Miller, translated by A. R. Price. Cambridge: Polity.

———. 2019 (1975). The Third." *The Lacanian Review* 7 (Spring): 83–109.

Lamennais, Hugues-Felicité Robert de. 1895 (1817). *Essay on Indifference in Matters of Religion.* Translated by Lord Stanley of Alderly. London: John McQueen.

Lardreau, Guy. 1993. *La Véracité: Essai d'une philosophie negative.* Paris: Verdier.

Laurent, Éric. 2016. *L'Envers de la biopolitique: Une Écriture pour la jouissance*. Paris: Navarin/Le Champ Freudien.

Lazarus, Sylvain, ed. 1993. *Politique et philosophie dans l'oeuvre de Louis Althusser*. Paris: Presses Universitaires de France.

Lévi-Strauss, Claude. 1966. *The Savage Mind*. Chicago: University of Chicago Press.

Lloyd, G. E. R. 1973. *Greek Science after Aristotle*. London: Chatto and Windus.

Mach, Ernst. 1988 (1883). *The Science of Mechanics: A Critical and Historical Account of Its Development*. Translated by T. J. McCormack, introduction by Karl Menger. La Salle, Ill.: Open Court.

Mallarmé, Stephane. 1994. "A Throw of the Dice." In *Collected Poems: A Bilingual Edition*, translated and with a commentary by Henry Weinfeld, 124–46. Berkeley: University of California Press.

Miller, Jacques-Alain. 1981. "Encyclopédie." *Ornicar?* 24: 35–44.

———. 2014. "L'Inconscient et le corps parlant." *La Cause du Désir* 88 (November): 104–14.

Milner, Jean-Claude. 1978. *L'Amour de la langue*. Paris: Le Seuil.

———. 1983. *Les Noms indistincts*. Paris: Le Seuil.

———. 1989. *Introduction à une science du langage*. Paris: Le Seuil.

———. 1990. *For the Love of Language*. Translated by Ann Banfield. New York: St. Martin's Press.

———. 1993. *Archéologie d'un échec, 1950–1993*. Paris: Le Seuil.

———. 2008 (2002). "Retour à Saussure." In *Le Périple structural: Figures et paradigme*, 15–43. Lagrasse, Fr.: Verdier/Poche.

———. 2017. "Back and Forth from Letter to Homophony." *Problemi International* 1, no. 1: 81–98.

———. 2019. "Lacan's Later Work and the *Declaration of the Rights of Man*." *The Lacanian Review* 7 (Spring): 202–8.

Norden, Eduard. 1898. *Die antieke Kunstprosa vom VI. Jahrhundert v. Chr. bis in die Zeit der Renaissance*. Leipzig: B. G. Teubner.

Ornicar? 1977. Issue no. 8, "L'Excommunication," edited by Jacques-Alain Miller. Paris.

Pascal, Blaise. 1995. *Pensées*. Translated by A. J. Krailsheimer. London: Penguin.

Plato. *Meno*. 1980. In *The Collected Dialogues*, edited by Edith Hamilton and Huntington Cairns, translated by W. K. C. Guthrie, 353–84. Princeton, N.J.: Princeton University Press.

———. *The Republic*. 1980. In *The Collected Dialogues*, edited by Edith Hamilton and Huntington Cairns, translated by Paul Shorey, 575–844. Princeton, N.J.: Princeton University Press.

———. *Timaeus*. 1980. In *The Collected Dialogues*, edited by Edith Hamilton and Huntington Cairns, translated by Benjamin Jowett, 1151–1211. Princeton, N.J.: Princeton University Press.

Queneau, Raymond. 1986. "The Relation X Takes Y for Z." In *Oulipo: A Primer of Potential Literature*, translated and edited by Warren F. Motte, Jr., 153–55. Normal, Ill.: Dalkey Archive.

Rabelais. 1900 (1653–94). *Gargantua and Pantagruel*, vol. 1. Translated by Sir

Thomas Urquhart and Peter Le Motteux, with an introduction by Charles Whibley. London: David Nutt.

Redondi, Pietro. 1987. *Galileo Heretic.* Translated by Raymond Rosenthal. Princeton, N.J.: Princeton University Press.

Regnault, François. 1985. *Dieu est inconscient: Études lacaniennes autour de saint Thomas d'Aquin.* Paris: Navarin.

———. 1992. "Traits de genie." In *Connaissez-vous Lacan?* by M.-P. de Cossé-Brissac et al., 219–30. Paris: Le Seuil.

Rosenbloom, Paul. 1950. *The Elements of Mathematical Logic.* New York: Dover.

Roubaud, Jacques. 1993. *L'Invention du fils de Leoprepes.* Paris: Circé.

Roudinesco, Élisabeth. 1990 (1986). *Jacques Lacan and Co.: A History of Psychoanalysis in France, 1925–1985.* Translated, with a foreword, by Jeffrey Mehlman. Chicago: University of Chicago Press.

———. 1997 (1994). *Jacques Lacan: Outline of a Life, History of a System of Thought.* Translated by Barbara Bay. New York: Columbia University Press.

Saussure, Ferdinand de. 1986 (1916). *Course in General Linguistics.* Edited by Charles Bally and Albert Sechehaye, with Albert Riedlinger, translated by Roy Harris. La Salle, Ill.: Open Court.

Scholz, Heinrich. 1961a. *Concise History of Logic.* New York: Philosophical Library.

———. 1961b (1930). "Die Axiomatik der Alten." In *Mathesis Universalis: Abhandlungen zur Philosophie als Strenger Wissenschaft,* edited by Hans Hermes, Friedrich Kambartel, and Joachim Ritter, 27–44. Basel/Stuttgart: Benno Schwabe.

———. 1961c (1943/44). "Einführung in die kantische Philosophie." In *Mathesis Universalis: Abhandlungen zur Philosophie als strenger Wissenschaft,* edited by Hans Hermes, Friedrich Kambartel, and Joachim Ritter, 152–218. Basel/Stuttgart: Benno Schwabe.

Serres, Michel. 2001 (1977). *The Birth of Physics.* Translated by David Webb and William Ross. London: Clinamen.

Simon, Gérard. 1988. *Le Regard, l'être, et l'apparence dans l'optique de l'antiquité.* Paris: Le Seuil.

Soulez, Antonia. 1985. Introduction to *Manifeste du cercle de Vienne et autres écrits.* Paris: Presses Universitaires de France.

Starobinski, Jean. 1979 (1971). *Words upon Words: The Anagrams of Ferdinand de Saussure.* Translated by Olivia Emmet. New Haven, Conn.: Yale University Press.

Strauss, Leo. 2013. *On Tyranny: Corrected and Expanded Edition, including the Strauss-Kojève Correspondence.* Edited by Victor Gourevitch and Michael S. Roth. *c*ago: University of Chicago Press.

·0. René Char en ses poèmes. Paris: Gallimard.

· L'Intuitionnisme kantien. Paris: Vrin.

·8 (1921). Tractatus Logico-Philosophicus. Translated by C. *·* Dover.